'What an amazing book! Crammed full of great advice and tips, all delivered simply and clearly, sprinkled with funny anecdotes. I'd recommend this to all parents looking to support their child in school and to all teachers who want to build a collaborative approach with pupils and parents.'
— *Richard Nurse, parent and founder of Picturepath*

'Debby and Gareth have combined their respective experiences as parent and professional to create a treasure trove of inclusive principles and practical strategies. Not only does this book offer hope to parents in overcoming various barriers, but for educators it provides a blueprint for an autism-friendly school based on understanding, proactivity, consistency and collaboration.'
— *Dr Chris Moore, educational psychologist*

'As an autistic person and someone whose doctoral research is focused around autism education within and outside the English educational context, I can't express enough how refreshing it is to read a book that champions the viewpoint of autistic people themselves. I'll definitely be recommending the book to colleagues.'
— *Jonathan Hays, Head of Inclusion and Learning Support,*
Concord Academy, Shanghai

'With excellent advice at every step, this book is a masterclass of collaboration and co-production that every secondary school could use as a template, all supported with the pupil voice at its heart. A truly collaborative title.'
— *Lynn McCann, autism specialist teacher, trainer and author*

'The authors have created a wonderful template for parents and educators to follow, allowing both parties to recognise the barriers faced by young autistic learners, advocate for them in education settings, and empower them to work together collaboratively to remove those barriers.'
— *Kieran Rose, autistic writer, trainer and consultant,*
www.theautisticadvocate.com

'I wish this book had been around when I moved up to "the big school". It brings together the experiences of a wise mum and an enlightened educator, dispensing friendly advice that should make all those involved in preparing an autistic teen for secondary school feel confident and empowered. A masterclass in a ng students to thrive.'
ura Campbell, co-author of
men: Autism and Parenting

'Reading this was a game-changer for us. Packed with "real-life" advice from authors who know how parents feel.'

– *Tracey Stanley, parent*

'Brimming with positivity, tried-and-tested tips and proactive strategies to facilitate authentic inclusion. This handbook is the perfect companion for any parent of an autistic young person as they journey through secondary school – and for the school staff who work with them.'

– *Dr Ruth Moyse, Director, AT-Autism*

'This is the most raw and honest, yet inspiring and hopeful book I've ever read in regards supporting your autistic child through mainstream education. A truly fabulous book.'

– *Shaunagh Kane, parent*

'Informally written, this book offers comprehensive, honest and practical advice for parents and professionals. A definite "must-have".'

– *Kath Lennon, assistant headteacher for SEND and inclusion, including autism lead teacher*

'A book to keep re-reading to remind ourselves of how to support one another and how to enhance our approaches collaboratively to really be inclusive. *Championing Your Autistic Teen at Secondary School* is brilliant.'

– *Elly Chapple, parent, Founder #FlipTheNarrative, TEDx speaker*

'An honest, well-written perspective combining pupil experiences, strategies, research, good practices and policies when considering mainstream education for secondary-age pupils. This book highlights the need for a school culture that predicts triggers and works in an inclusive manner by being proactive rather than reactive.'

– *Taneisha Pascoe-Matthews, assistant headteacher/ SENCo and mother of two autistic boys*

'A vibrant, knowing and pragmatic resource for parents and schools, this is a highly readable companion for the journey to secondary school founded on principles of respect and relationship.'

– *Barney Angliss, education consultant and trainer, former SENCo and mentor to autistic teens*

CHAMPIONING YOUR AUTISTIC TEEN AT SECONDARY SCHOOL

Getting the Best from Mainstream Settings

DEBBY ELLEY
with GARETH D. MOREWOOD

Foreword by Peter Vermeulen
Illustrated by Terry Culkin

Jessica Kingsley Publishers
London and Philadelphia

First published in Great Britain in 2022 by Jessica Kingsley Publishers
An imprint of Hodder & Stoughton Ltd
An Hachette UK Company

1

A CIP catalogue record for this title is available from the
British Library and the Library of Congress

ISBN 978 1 83997 074 0
eISBN 978 1 83997 075 7

Printed and bound in Great Britain by CPI Group

Jessica Kingsley Publishers' policy is to use papers that are natural, renewable and recyclable products and made from wood grown in sustainable forests. The logging and manufacturing processes are expected to conform to the environmental regulations of the country of origin.

Jessica Kingsley Publishers
Carmelite House
50 Victoria Embankment
London EC4Y 0DZ

www.jkp.com

Contents

Foreword

In June 1994, more than 300 representatives of almost 100 governments and 25 international disability and education organisations gathered in the beautiful city of Salamanca, some 200 kilometres west of Madrid, Spain. They attended the World Conference on Special Needs Education, organised by the Government of Spain in collaboration with the UNESCO. At the end of the conference, the delegates agreed on a statement, now known as the Salamanca Statement. This statement states that mainstream schools should accommodate all children, regardless of their physical or mental conditions. Inclusion should be the norm. Children with a disability should be able to attend the school of their choice in their neighbourhood, the school they would attend if they did not have a special condition or disability.

The main reason for drawing the card of inclusion is that an inclusive orientation is the most effective way for building an inclusive society, a society that leaves no one behind. Moreover, inclusive education might improve the efficiency and ultimately the cost-effectiveness of the education system. This line of thought and the call for inclusion was repeated in 2015, when the United Nations put inclusive education forward as one of the 17 sustainable development goals for 2030.

There is now scientific evidence that inclusive education fosters social inclusion in the long term. Inclusive education increases the opportunities for peer connection and friendships between students with and without disabilities. Students with a disability who attended mainstream schools have better social and academic outcomes, and are more likely to be employed and financially independent.

Despite this evidence and the worldwide call for inclusive action, inclusion of students with special educational needs and disabilities is still more a dream than reality. The recommendations are well ahead of practice throughout much of the world. This is especially the case for autistic learners.

When it comes to inclusive education of autistic children and youngsters, there is a lot of goodwill in the best case and tokenism in the worst case. There are not many schools that openly refuse children on the autism spectrum. Many schools say they are accepting autistic students and they commit to inclusion. But anyone who has talked to parents of autistic children has heard numerous examples of exclusion. A survey in 2016 of almost 1000 parents by the National Autistic Society showed that nearly one child in five had received at least one temporary exclusion. One-third of the parents reported that their child had been informally excluded at least once.

And then there are the hidden exclusions, such as students taking part in the normal programme but being excluded from school trips, students being physically present in the classroom but not actively involved in group or classroom activities. Autistic children are more likely to be bullied than those with other or no special needs. And even if they are not bullied, they are more likely to be isolated or on the periphery of the social world at school. Teachers, parents and students all report poorer student–teacher relationships with less closeness and more conflict and misunderstandings.

Not a very uplifting story, is it? Before you start ordering antidepressants, here's the good news. Yes, inclusive education of autistic students is more fiction than fact, but in my 35 years of work in the autism field I've seen the attitude toward inclusive education of autistic children and youngsters change for the better. It still needs to grow a lot, but neurodiversity is becoming more accepted now than ten years ago, when almost no one had even heard about the term.

Parents want their autistic children to be included and given equal chances for learning and developing. More and more schools want to include autistic children and give them the quality of education they deserve.

Maybe I am a bit naïve or I am suffering from an illusion, but I am convinced that anno 2022 there is enough goodwill and plenty of good intentions. At least more than when I entered the autism field in the 1980s, when autistic children were seen by many teachers and principals almost as aliens with a lot of strange and challenging behaviours.

The thing is, good intentions alone will not get you very far. What is needed is knowledge about strategies to realise inclusion in practice. Practical tips to ensure that autistic children can thrive at school and that they love to go to school. There's a lot of goodwill; what is lacking is know-how.

And that is why this book is such a precious gift. It does not offer a complicated academic analysis of all the possible difficulties and barriers that can pop up when an autistic student goes to school. Instead, it offers a wealth of useful and easily applicable tips. Tips that come from a lived experience with autism, a thorough knowledge of how autistic students experience the world in general and school in particular and – above all – a respect for all parties in the inclusion story: the student, the parents and the teachers. Creating an autism-friendly school is not a mission impossible. On the contrary, many of the tips in this book are easy to use. And it is not only the autistic student who will benefit from them, but also other students. I've said it already a zillion times in my lectures for teachers and schools: an autism-friendly school is identical to a student-friendly school. And teachers have a less tough job when all their students feel good. So, it's a win-win for everyone!

The authors of this book, Debby and Gareth, radiate an air of optimism, practical common sense and, above all, a belief that successful inclusion of autistic children can be achieved. Gareth and Debby offer an invaluable guide that can help parents, teachers and school staff to answer the call for inclusion made some 25 years ago by the large group of representatives who gathered in sunny Salamanca.

Peter Vermeulen

Acknowledgements

First, thanks to Debby's son Bobby, who was responsible for the authors meeting in the first place and then working successfully together as parent and practitioner at his secondary school. Through many meetings, many cups of tea and (too) many bad jokes, we found our common ground!

We would also like to thank the researchers, authors and education practitioners who have provided us with so much valuable material for this book. Particular thanks to Neil Humphrey, Judith Hebron and Wendy Symes, for the work that they've done in the education field. We are also very grateful to photographer Alfie Bowen for sharing his personal experiences of school in the name of changing things for the better.

A big cheer for all of the parents, carers and families who shared their experiences, good and bad, with us. Some of those experiences haven't made it directly into this book, but they have all informed it.

A huge 'Cheers – we owe you!' to artist Terry Culkin for his witty illustrations.

Finally, thanks to every parent, carer and teacher who takes the time and trouble to buy or borrow this book (oh and yes, to read it!). Throughout our collaborations as parent and professional and in writing this book, we realise we don't agree on everything and sometimes start from quite different viewpoints. However, we have always found a way forward through common ground, so we really hope that you take from this some advice and information from our own journey that will help bring about positive change for you, whatever your role or circumstance.

Notes on the Text

COMMON TERMS USED THROUGHOUT THIS BOOK
Person first or identity first?
We refer to your 'autistic child' rather than 'child with autism'. Opinions vary but in our own experience autistic people generally prefer that their autism is acknowledged as part of who they are. We generally assume that you know we are referring to autism and sometimes just use the words child, youngster or teen.

'Behaviour'
You may have noticed that we have consistently avoided the term 'behaviour' when talking about autism. Unfortunately, this word has gradually developed in conversation to mean 'problematic stuff'; we prefer to reframe that debate around stress and stressors.

We want to avoid mixing up the daily mannerisms, habits and coping strategies that are just a part of being autistic with the unwanted side effects that arise as a result of challenges outweighing coping resources. And by the way, when we say 'unwanted', we mean both on the part of the staff member and the person experiencing it. No one enjoys feeling so distressed that they're out of control. The emphasis therefore is on minimising stress rather than 'behaviours'.

Other terms

EHCP – Education, Health and Care Plan

SALT – Speech and Language Therapist

SENCo – Special Educational Needs Coordinator

SEN – Special Educational Needs

SEND – Special Educational Needs and Disability

TA – Teaching Assistant

Preface

As co-founder and co-editor of the parenting magazine *AuKids*, Debby Elley had the idea for this book after receiving numerous e-mails from parents and carers asking for advice relating to their children's mainstream schooling.

Many of these families were experiencing conflict with school staff, were distressed that their children's wellbeing was being affected by poor practice and wanted to know how best to approach disagreements and improve outcomes.

As a parent of autistic teenagers herself, Debby was used to writing about good collaboration, helping carers to identify strategies for success at school and advising them on how to handle conflict.

However, in order to bring additional perspectives to this advice, she needed a co-author who was experienced in inclusive education. Enter stage left...Gareth D. Morewood!

Gareth already knew Debby. As both Special Education Needs Coordinator (SENCo) and Director of Curriculum Support at her son's mainstream school, he had not only been instrumental in creating an inclusive environment there, but also been involved in ground-breaking research studies on inclusion practice. Gareth was very much 'walking the walk' and being an active agent of change within the provision for Debby's son.

Gareth now works as an education adviser and trainer with schools both in the UK and abroad, introducing them to the pioneering Saturation Model (Chapter 8), which ensures that a school culture develops in ways that merge both policy and practice for successful inclusion at every level. He also supports culture change through the LASER programme, which he jointly developed with Professor Andy McDonnell. More about that later in this book!

Gareth has dedicated his career to helping schools understand what it takes to be truly inclusive. Debby has dedicated her career to helping parents become effective advocates for their autistic children.

Together, we hope to create a book that will improve your child's mainstream experience at secondary school.

However, we both know that the world isn't perfect. Although our own parent–professional collaboration has worked well, there are different kinds of challenges in every mainstream setting.

Some secondary schools have a great understanding of what they need to do to support autistic learners and an equally positive relationship with parents and carers.

Some don't. Indeed, every setting is unique.

As a result of non-inclusive practice, carers can find themselves in a long, exhausting battle with their teenager's education setting.

When the working relationship between family and school fails, there's the painful and drawn-out process of switching settings. Unfortunately, local authorities aren't always supportive of this decision and the whole scenario becomes stressful, often including lawyers and mediation services.

However, we have a big problem. We have a lot of schools that don't quite 'get' autism, and a lot of disillusioned pupils switching between them. Sometimes even the switch doesn't mean positive progress, and autistic pupils end up feeling like failures, their confidence destroyed, leaving a trail of schools behind them.

The saddest news of all is that carers follow exhausted in their wake, their parenting energy depleted by endless rows with education settings. They need that energy and they need it badly.

This can't be left to happen. So we thought we might be able to do something to help, in a small way, with this book.

If our writing here improves the outcomes for one young person, it will have been time well spent. If we can support more families and schools, we'd be truly happy.

Schools need better resources, training and management when it comes to SEND: there's no question of this.

But take a deep breath.

Although this is a sorry state of affairs, there is some hope on the horizon. *All* schools – no matter how experienced in working with autistic learners and their families or how poorly funded – can definitely adapt their practices.

In this book, we aim to help you choose the right school and to build fantastic collaboration right from the start. We'll address common barriers for autistic pupils and share how the best schools overcome them. We'll also give you the skills to head off conflict at the earliest opportunity and coach you to build a productive working relationship with your child's setting.

We can't promise that as a result of this book a non-inclusive school with an inflexible culture will suddenly become an all-singing, all-dancing autism utopia.

Nor are we promising that having read this book, you will magically find that every conflict is beautifully resolved to your satisfaction. We hope, however, you'll find some elements that will prove useful and helpful.

So, what are we going to deliver instead?

★ By the end of this book you'll be well versed in common hurdles faced by autistic pupils in mainstream settings.

★ You'll read about great, proven strategies for overcoming them.

★ You'll be shown how to start and maintain a good parent/carer–teacher collaboration and how to handle problems in a way that will give you the best chance of reaching an agreement.

★ You'll learn how to communicate difficulties in ways that will encourage a productive response.

★ You'll learn how the best settings cope with challenges, and you'll be ready to inspire your own setting with similar ideas.

★ If conflict persists, we'll tell you what next steps you should take.

In a far from perfect world, this book may just help you to tip the balance in your child's favour – and that's good news for education settings, for carers and, most importantly, for students themselves.

Finally, a bit of advice before we start! Good results take a little effort. Don't fret, it's not exactly the sort of effort that requires digging a tunnel with a teaspoon, but you'll be required to communicate with school perhaps more than other teenagers' parents. We'd far rather you made the small effort of communicating little and often, rather than having to make the gigantic effort of responding to a crisis. Makes sense, doesn't it?

Take time to digest each chapter. Pace yourself to give yourself a good chance of being able to use the advice, and try to avoid reading it when you're stressed or under pressure, when we know that you may be inclined to skip some important sections. That's because we've been there and done the same!

Oh, and if you are part of a partnership caring for a child, please do yourself a favour and pass this book around. Getting great ideas is one thing, but it's generally laborious having to recall them all for the benefit of others. Reading a paragraph out loud while someone else is glued to the TV isn't quite the same as having them read it themselves. It will stand you in good stead if everyone has read the same advice.

We wish your child a positive, fruitful secondary school education – and hope that this book helps you to achieve that in some small way!

In order for people to know who we really are, we have to be able to show our true colours. How can people understand autism if they never see it?

Bobby Elley, age 18

CHAPTER 1

FINDING THE 'PERFECT' SETTING

Here's the thing – there isn't one! There are, hmm, let's see...yes, zero mainstream schools that are completely perfect for autistic children.

Why?

It's due to the fact that the entire education system is designed to cram an enormous amount of information into a short space of time, at the end of which are a series of exams. In order to convince teenage pupils who feel less than motivated to work for these exams, a certain amount of panic-inducing rhetoric is often used.

Although this may work for some, for the more anxious among the student population – including autistic children – this is a system built around far too much pressure.

Added to that, most secondary schools (in the UK at least) can be home to a population of roughly a thousand pupils or more.

That's a thousand teenagers with raging hormones and a lot to prove to their peers. Interactions aren't gentle and tactful; they're full-on and sometimes confrontational. Usually when teenagers come across someone who is different, they don't take too much time to consider how their words are landing before they loudly and rudely point this out in the most offensive way possible.

And then, into this sprawling metropolis of hormones, young egos and unsympathetic loudmouths, you place your 11-year-old autistic youngster. Sometimes they're in a different place, socially. With definite academic capabilities, they also have limitations on what they can process and in what sort of environment they can process it.

Basically, schools are not designed around autistic children; historically, autistic children have had to fit into these poorly designed systems, so from the start there are even more challenges for them than their peers are faced with.

Anything can tip the balance between a good and a bad day. There's academic challenges, there are social ones, there are sensory ones, there are changes in routine, unclear instructions and ambiguous language...and then there's the different contexts in which all these take place.

These challenges are different on every day of the week, and from week to week. Being able to 'cope' one day doesn't mean you can the next. Many factors including sleep and general health can mean you have fewer coping strategies one day compared with the next. This is often a big challenge in schools, where the old mantra 'Well, you managed that okay last week...' rings out.

Stress (caused by a number of factors) accompanies your youngster like a crow on their shoulder, which can be amplified with their diagnosis.

They've just crawled to the top of the mountain in their first school. Proudly, they've been able to survey the ground below, enjoying the kudos of being the oldest in the school.

And now here they are. The youngest, the smallest, starting from scratch once more.

Understandably, parents and carers are extremely anxious themselves when applying for secondary schools. Why do we even put ourselves through it?

The simple answer is that we have little choice. In our system, there's special school, sometimes a separate unit within mainstream, a mainstream school or home education. Considering the many ways we have of experiencing learning, our system is essentially a narrow one, with limited flexibility and centrally controlled definitions of success. Too often, young people are forced to 'normalise' in a setting designed without them in mind; this in essence is the main challenge faced.

We'd like to point out that there are some welcome and notable exceptions to this landscape. We'll be giving examples throughout this book of where things have worked differently. In addition, some forward thinkers are starting to create different education experiences: smaller, highly specialist environments designed for autistic learners who are academically able but fare better in a bespoke setting dedicated to supporting learning differences. Note – these are differences, not disabilities. Don't assume your area doesn't have one; it pays to look.

However, the system in general is not geared towards the minority cohort of autistic children and to be honest probably never will be... although it could do a darn sight better than it's doing at the moment.

Considering all of this, you can see why even a very good mainstream school isn't exactly a natural environment for autistic youngsters.

With all that said, when you look around a school, let's be clear that there are some choices that are better than others – massively so, in fact!

SO WHAT SHOULD YOU LOOK FOR?

Well, you may not like this, but we believe you should never choose a secondary school based on the sole argument that *all their friends are going there*.

We know you might find that difficult to read.

It's true that your child won't entirely embrace being separated from kids who give them a sense of stability.

However, a couple of things to point out here. First, if the chosen school isn't inclusive and can't be adequately flexible and understanding around your youngster's needs, then no amount of friendships will be able to balance out the amount of stress they'll experience.

Second, children change hugely within the first few years of secondary school. There's no guarantee that best bud in Year 5 will remain best bud in Year 8, and in fact that growing rift can be accompanied by its own anguish.

Different cliques form, kids grow apart, and you can't promise that these primary school buddies will be your child's safe place to fall just because they are in attendance at the same education setting. They may not even be in the same classes or cross paths from one day to the next.

Choose the setting for reasons other than existing friendships – and then not only will your child still keep their true, loyal buddies for holidays and weekends, but they'll also form new friendships in secondary school.

Without friendships being your first consideration, other factors need to take centre stage.

At the end of this book (see Appendix 1: Useful Charts) is a checklist for when you are considering schools. We wouldn't recommend filling it in at the time; it might prevent you from listening properly and it may be off-putting to those showing you around. However, setting aside time to reflect and complete the form after each visit may highlight missing areas – a useful benchmark.

Be confident that a good response, just as much as a very poor one, will stay in your mind until you get home. And if you cannot recall something mentioned at all, it is likely that it wasn't, so you can follow up with an email or phone call...or add it to a list of reasons never to return!

By all means modify our questions as you think best; ensuring an approach personalised to your child's needs is important.

Don't purely rely on answers to your pertinent questions, though. Here are some other tips to help you separate the clued-up from the clueless:

PRE-VISIT DETECTIVE WORK

Exam results aren't everything. Read what parents or carers of children with special educational needs and disabilities (SEND) say about the school. Does the school appear to have a good relationship with them? If you can, speak to another parent who has an autistic pupil at the school. Is there a local parent/carer or families' group you can contact?

Sometimes these families are quoted in Ofsted reports and you can look at Ofsted's Parent View section, too. A word of caution, however: often the most positive comments are not routinely recorded there, and sometimes a school with a lower inspection grade can in fact be a great match for your child. It most certainly isn't a binary choice here.

Have a look at the school's website. Every school in England must have an Information Report outlining SEND provision on their website – this is statutory, so if you can't find it within three clicks, drop in an email and ask for it directly in advance of any visit.

What does the report (and other parts of the website) say about adapting for pupils with SEND? Does the website show pupils of different abilities engaged in different activities? Is the language inclusive and welcoming?

Finally, take a look at the school policies online, in particular those to do with behaviour, bullying and SEND. Under the Equality Act 2010 (UK), schools in the United Kingdom are obliged to be proactive in overcoming barriers to equal access and participation. Is there any evidence that this school is proud of having done this?

Can you see the voices of young people easily enough? Are families' views presented as part of a community, or it is very much the setting *telling* you what they do and how you *must* engage with them?

PROACTIVE VERSUS REACTIVE SCHOOLS

In order for a school to have an inclusive culture, policies combine with practice to ensure that the school is *proactive* rather than *reactive* when it comes to making learning fully accessible to pupils with special needs.

Proactive schools form strategies and procedures based on a good knowledge of each individual and their potential difficulties. A proactive school might reassure you during a chat by giving you some examples of other children who have different challenges with the environment – and telling you what they have in place around their needs.

By contrast, *reactive* schools have a piecemeal approach to problem-solving and adopt knee-jerk strategies as and when there's an issue. In answer to your questions about potential difficulties, you may get a 'we'll cross that bridge if and when we come to it' style answer. Red light!

Reactive schools will be less effective at creating a calm and inclusive atmosphere, because (to use an analogy) rather than recognising that a bomb is likely to explode if a match is lit next to it, they wait for the first bomb to explode and then hold a meeting about what to do when they find a second one.

Proactive schools are easy to spot – there will be tonnes of examples of where procedures are slightly tweaked in line with pupils' needs – children might be able to borrow iPads to help with recording, go somewhere quieter during lunch, have a more flexible timetable... You're looking for examples of flexibility without fuss and a listening ear.

> *Proactive schools are easy to spot – there will be tonnes of examples of where procedures are slightly tweaked in line with pupils' needs.*

Plus – this sounds obvious but it's a dead giveaway – think about whether you are made to feel welcome. It's usually pretty obvious from the attitude of those you meet if autistic children are viewed as a burden and a cost.

Do you get the sense that your child will be expected to fit into their way of doing things, or do you get a sense that the school will adapt and be flexible around your child's needs?

One key thing to look out for is whether they refer to the youngster by name or simply by their diagnosis. A 'red flag' for us is language like 'this is what we do for autistic children...'. Knowing what is going to be in place for *your* child is key, rather than one-size-fits-all strategies that are likely to miss key individual requirements, having been informed by decades-old, outdated training.

MESSAGES: PUNITIVE, INSPIRING...INCLUSIVE?

Read the types of messages that pupils are given in communications around the school, too. They can be great clues as to the school's ethos. Debby visited a school once where every poster seemed to publicise warnings of behaviour sanctions. She didn't return.

THE PEOPLE

Expertise in special and additional needs is a very good sign that the school prioritises them. Try to spot whether you have a lone SENCo wandering around without support, or whether there is a SEND team that includes staff at management level, as part of the Senior Leadership Team (you can look for this on the website in advance of any visit).

It's great if you're able to meet autistic pupils, too – and hear their assessment of the school. In Gareth's school, autistic pupils conducted the tour for prospective families. For the school, supporting pupils in planning the route and listening to what they said often provided an additional way to find out more about their views of the school as well!

THE ATTITUDE

There are three main things that a school needs in order to be a great choice – and believe it or not, none of those things involves extra money:

1. the willingness and ability to communicate with you, to listen and learn

2. the willingness and ability to be flexible and adaptable

3. a focus on solutions and what your child *can* do, not what they *can't*.

If school staff are willing to listen to you and work with you to tailor their approaches to suit your child's needs, they don't have to be autism experts in order to be effective (in fact, no one is truly an autism expert – that's a myth). After all, the expert on your child is you; great schools utilise this as part of real collaboration. Usually, however, they will have a degree of knowledge within school as they will be welcoming other autistic children, too.

DANGER SIGNS

In any school, there are red flags telling you whether they're inclusive or not; you just have to be savvy enough to spot them. Here's our list of signs that should make you wary.

★ No one from a learning support team shows you around and you don't meet the SENCo.

★ The school is so proud of itself that someone you meet drones on about the (one) autistic child they taught who did very well, yet they never ask about your child.

★ The school greets you enthusiastically as a parent or carer but throughout the meeting never asks your child for their thoughts or opinions.

★ Posters around the school are centred around behaviour and work warnings and sanctions; they have a punitive tone rather than showing pictures of success and good news stories.

★ Your information regarding autism difficulties is greeted with indifference, generic 'we do this...' statements or dismissive responses.

★ The only playgrounds are the large ones where all pupils congregate with no smaller ones overseen by staff. There's no mention about quiet areas away from the main body of the school.

★ Similarly, there is only one large canteen and no alternatives; adjustments regarding navigating lunchtimes are dismissed.

★ There is nowhere for pupils to retreat to if they feel over-whelmed or any mention of key procedures or key adults when stressors become overwhelming.

GREAT SIGNS

We also have some green flags to help spot the opposite:

★ Your child is greeted enthusiastically and listened to attentively and respectfully, even when they aren't at their most articulate.

★ There is flexibility with the curriculum; the school is prepared to adapt and reduce a full timetable to suit a child's needs, allowing for homework, 'down time' or revision during the day and some respite from lessons. Pre-learning is also a consideration – that is, preparing children for learning by introducing them to unfamiliar words and concepts to look at before a new lesson on a topic.

★ Posters around school reflect diversity and inclusion and share positive 'can do' stories.

★ There is evidence of anti-bullying (and other) policies and pupil involvement in them.

★ You are listened to seriously when you talk about difficulties and then staff communicate practical solutions that are tried and tested at school, while also being open to new and innovative possibilities that may have never been used before.

★ There are a variety of quiet places to retreat to at unstructured times, some of them with staff present. Access to these is explained clearly and without complexity.

★ Pupils are accustomed to using equipment and technology to overcome difficulties (e.g. pupils are allowed to type rather than write); there are many who use reader pens (text-to-speech scanners for dyslexic learners) routinely and so on.

★ The pupils who show you around aren't just obvious high-flyers or extroverts.

★ Pupils and adults are genuinely welcoming to your child when you are looking around.

★ Staff are happy to show you the 'hub' areas where SEND pupils can go to work or rest; they explain how they operate clearly.

SHOWSTOPPER SIGNS

It is time to get out the party poppers if you observe these on top of other good signs:

★ Pupils with SEND have been encouraged to take on positions of responsibility, such as involvement in clubs and pupil forums, helping out in the library, as prefects, etc.

★ Pupils with SEND have personalised learning areas that they can retreat to in a quiet place, ideally as part of a planned, personalised timetable.

★ Inset days include regular staff updates and training on SEND and all staff (especially reception/office/site staff you meet on arrival) are welcoming.

★ People smile and seem genuinely happy!

ASKING QUESTIONS

Don't be shy about asking questions. If your youngster is going to spend all week nearly every week in this place, it's vital that they feel safe and included. Ask questions not purely to get information but to watch the reaction. Awkwardness or evasiveness suggests that they aren't used to such questions and probably not set up to meet these challenges when they arise.

A vague answer suggests that they're glossing over a lack of provision. A school that has great autism provision will be only too willing to answer every question in detail, or at least show an interest in developing better provision – or, perhaps most importantly, say they don't know or would need to work with you and your child to develop something new.

You'd be hard pressed to find a school that ticks every box. If you're looking for the perfect provision, as we said at the beginning of this chapter, you're unlikely to find it, unless the headteacher is some sort of autism magician.

However, your questions will give you a general feel for whether a school is going to work with you or against you; listing pros and cons and your *sense* of a place is important when making considerations (never ignore a gut feeling!).

Additionally, even if the provision doesn't feel right, but there is a genuine willingness to work with you and your child, it might in fact be just right for you. One thing is for sure: partnerships are vital, so if you don't feel you would have those with key staff, that could limit possibilities and will help you to make that all-important decision.

Too many parents sign up for the wrong school and then regret it, when the danger signs were there from the first visit. Similarly, it is easy to dismiss a great setting on one factor or a small thing; with flexibility and staff who listen, a school that isn't well versed in autism may become great because of your child being there.

One last thing, when you're looking at schools, compare like for like. Ask the same questions of each and note the responses (if not at the time, then afterwards). Note also your first impressions and think about your plan beforehand, as follow-up questions and additional visits may be difficult, depending upon your timeframe.

Some people can get a bit carried away with loving a school and not put it through any rigorous quality control! Or you can find the member of staff slightly hurried and intimidating and be put off finishing your list of questions. Well, don't be put off. You've got every right to check these things. Thinking in advance and bringing another family member or friend with you can be important additional supports.

Once you have got all your answers, you can make yourself a lovely homemade chart of all the schools against their answers.

If anyone wants to know why you've asked for a certain setting, you then have a watertight, evidence-based argument of the needs that were and weren't met by each. This information can be invaluable, so it's definitely worth gathering it up at the time to have it ready as required.

Believe us, you can quickly forget details or get mixed up between settings. The chart will be your friend when it comes to applications.

INCLUDING YOUR CHILD

It's important that you obtain your child's early 'buy-in' for the choice of secondary school, as it will raise their confidence and help them to feel more in control.

Before you make a decision, ask them what's most important to them about school. This may need to be started early so that you can develop a list of important things to them and chat through what currently helps them in their primary setting.

Hypothetical questions about the future don't work well for autistic children. Instead, focus on what's worked for them in the past. Ask them these sorts of questions:

* ★ What have you liked best about school so far?

* ★ What helps you to feel relaxed at school?

* ★ What things make you feel nervous at school?

Show them that you are making a note of their views and questions, and they'll be part of your decision-making. Sometimes sending these questions from your child in advance to the school allows for a more positive experience, especially if other pupils can address their concerns and questions on a peer-to-peer level.

Here's the thing: most autistic kids only know that their parents or carers have chosen a secondary school for them when they are told the news 'You're going to XYZ School'.

When families tell us that their children are highly anxious about the secondary school transition, it's usually at this stage.

Bold statements along the lines of 'You're going to this school; it's been decided' are like a brick wall to many autistic young people. They speak of a future full of unknowns with no way out. That fuels anxiety and stress. The key to this is to reduce stressors, rather than adding to them.

Of course, your child isn't in a position to make the full decision themselves; nevertheless, we would strongly recommend that you approach this a little differently.

As you're going through the process of deciding on a school, explain your thinking to your child, involving them (however you can) in the process.

For instance, you could ask: 'What would you say if I gave a school a big tick if it has quiet places to go when you need a break from the noise? That's because you told me that you are more relaxed when you can have a rest from other people.'

Allow time to digest – processing time is often so important. Ask if they agree. They might add some suggestions of their own at that point.

The secondary school decision may be the first time that your child is truly aware of you making a decision on their behalf.

It's also important for their learning that they understand these three things about decision-making:

1. It's the best you can do, rather than perfection

People make decisions based on the best information they have available at the time. We can never guarantee a perfect decision because we don't know what the future holds, but we can give ourselves the best chance of a good decision.

We do this by gathering lots of information. This is what you've done – and you are showing this by taking notes on what is important to your child and highlighting also what you know is important to you. It is often very healthy for autistic children to learn that there is no such thing as a bulletproof, watertight, 100% solid-gold decision!

2. It's not irreversible

If the decision turns out to be misguided and the school doesn't suit your child, you will have the option to move. We realise that often choices are limited and battles required to secure appropriate placements, but being clear with your child is essential as part of this process.

3. The best bet is people who listen

Explain that one of the most important things to you is teachers who listen. So even if things *do* go wrong sometimes (and this happens in even the best schools), you have chosen a school where teachers will talk, listen and work things out together with you and your child. This collaborative approach is likely the most important element in the process, and if it is truly about positive relationships, almost anything can be addressed.

Often parents fret that they've reassured their child that things will be fine, when they don't even know themselves whether they will be. All you can do is teach them what an informed decision looks like. You can't nail down the future – this is life! Including them in the process and making them aware of your reasoning (in simple terms) shows them how good decisions are made.

So, the first day of high school is coming up.

How on earth do you prepare for that?

TIPS

- Don't forget to use our checklist for choosing an inclusive secondary school – you'll find it in Appendix 1: Useful Charts at the end of this book!

- If you need help searching for a school and making an appropriate choice, or if suitable settings seem thin on the ground, the advice on this page of the IPSEA (Independent Provider of Special Education Advice) website offers some very helpful guidance for those in England: www.ipsea. org.uk/choosing-a-schoolcollege-with-an-ehc-plan. If you aren't resident in England, or if you're interested in an independent setting, it's worth approaching them first to chat about admissions, as they may well support you.

CHAPTER 2

TRANSITION PREPARATION

By the time your child reaches the age of nine, you'll already be well versed in planning and preparation.

One thing you'll no doubt have learnt by now is that where autism is concerned, preparation is the key to reducing anxiety – for everyone!

PREPARING YOUR CHILD

When it comes to secondary school preparation, we advise you to start early, with a kind of 'drip-feed' approach.

There's a reason for this. If you suddenly bombard your child with information during the summer holidays before term begins, they're likely to get overwhelmed and highly anxious. It's generally preferable to spread out that information over a long period of time, allowing them to gradually become acclimatised to the idea of the new setting. But you know your child, so adapt this accordingly.

The Year 5 Transition Review is a key time for discussions and planning to start.

Like a lot of autistic children, Debby's son Bobby had a fear of things coming to an end. At the end of each year, he'd be in a slight panic when 31st December turned into 1st January. It was as if he saw the end of year as a cliff from which there was no return.

We helped Bobby to overcome this uncomfortable sensation by describing time as a wheel rather than something linear. The months and the seasons move on but are repeated annually; they come round again rather than simply stopping.

In much the same way, secondary school can just be seen as another part of their education, a wheel that keeps turning.

As the time for change nears, talk about the main differences between primary school and secondary school. Talk about them in a neutral way – for every change, there might be a drawback, essentially because it's new. But can they think of something positive about that change, too?

WORKING WITH PRIMARY SCHOOL STAFF

It's a great idea to plan for transition early, alongside your child's school staff. Although the statutory Transition Review in England takes place in Year 5, you'll know what is best for your child. Sometimes having small conversations earlier and building up discussions can work well.

However you approach it personally, make sure that you meet with the new school to discuss the plan. The focus should be on the key aspects of your child's schooling that will change when it comes to secondary school and what can reasonably be done to ensure that the change doesn't feel too dramatic.

If your last experience of secondary school was your own, visiting and getting a 'feel' for what things are currently like will be pretty important.

Planning a gradual increase of your child's independence will certainly help. For instance, if they've always delivered messages in school with a teaching assistant (TA), maybe they could go with a peer instead? Encouraging independence while in familiar and secure surroundings is a good time to start developing those skills.

PREPARING NEW STAFF

One of the best gifts you can give any child (or anyone, for that matter) is preparation. Visits and photographs are vital – as well as getting a timetable as early as you can.

However, as we're sure you know, it's not just about preparing your child. It's also about preparing the new staff.

Official paperwork obviously helps with this, outlining your child's specific needs.

Do ensure that you read any documentation that is produced after you've been given a draft of it – this is usually the Education, Health and Care Plan (EHCP) and associated reports.

Although it's a bureaucratic nuisance to read every line, we've been aware of rushed wording that's been misleading or lost in translation because of people misinterpreting what has been said at a meeting. This can cause significant issues further down the line. Clarifying early is important in getting off to a good start.

It's the SENCo's job to distil key facts from any documents for teaching staff and ensure that a whole-school approach is coordinated, so ensuring clarity and good communication between you and your child's new SENCo is vital.

However, preparation isn't just about legal paperwork. Considering what you and your family need is important and most definitely worth considering before any meetings and discussions.

Also, a SENCo, learning support team and TA might well be familiar with any legal plans that accompany your child to secondary school in their official paperwork. Great.

But it's difficult to imagine that the rest of the teaching staff will be spending long nights poring over the details of a child's education plan.

Your child may have a TA who's brilliant at translating needs to all teaching staff, or great staff who are particularly motivated to find out what your child's needs are. However, as our experience supporting other families and schools demonstrates, we wouldn't rely on this delightful scenario.

So, let's make sure that the new school is fully equipped.

THE CLASSROOM TIPS CHART

As Debby's son completed his final years at primary school, she and her son's TA developed a classroom tips chart (see Appendix 1: Useful Charts at the back of this book).

The chart simply showed specific difficulties that Bobby had experienced and which approaches worked best. Simple as that. Notes were made in this chart every time an accommodation or adaptation was made for Bobby.

Sometimes this chart was just a question of putting into words the sorts of approaches that Debby and the school had started to take for granted.

For instance, in the early years of primary school, Bobby's TA found that if she threw a blanket over the computer and said it was having a rest, this became non-confrontational speak for 'the computer is unavailable right now' – much less aggravating than 'you can't have it'.

There was also guidance on preparing for change, busy environments and handling other stressful situations. These weren't lengthy notes, just key pointers. There was a further column for long-term goals, in the cases where independence was being developed.

It's worth keeping a copy of this chart on your computer, so that you can update it as your youngster matures. Any strategy will develop over time and some may cease to be needed – hurrah for that!

There are several advantages to creating a classroom tips chart. First, when you're in a nurturing early years environment, you do tend to become oblivious to some accommodations that are made for your child and have become second nature. Staff know them well and get used to their 'little ways'.

Yet the usual way things are done in one setting may seem quite alien to another.

In addition, when secondary school staff ask, 'Anything we need to know?', it can be tricky to remember. Asked to come up with examples, your brain floats through some general scenarios but maybe finds it hard to identify lots of specific situations. By making notes as you go along during the last few years of primary school, you have a brilliant record evidencing good practice with particular obstacles.

From the secondary school's viewpoint, getting such information is amazingly helpful in planning and discussing transition with the young person and the family. Such information is never wasted, according to Gareth, and always useful.

The second advantage of the chart-making strategy is that it's in tabular form, which means that you have an at-a-glance guide, rather than a long-winded report. Oh, how we hate long-winded reports!

This classroom tips chart was used as an appendix to Bobby's official EHCP.

And, of course, things didn't stop there.

Call me cynical, comments Debby, but I didn't think that staff would be anxious to read EHCP appendices, so a copy of the chart was emailed to Gareth (who was Bobby's SENCo in waiting!), as well as Bobby's new secondary school form tutor, asking that she passed it on to his teachers. Additionally, ensuring his brand new TA had the information was an important starting point.

This was done as soon as the key personnel were known – and both sides agreed to make email addresses readily available. It was most definitely a 'great minds moment' as both school and home felt this was equally important.

Now, if you're not bored yet, let us give you another tip.

POINTERS, NOT DEMANDS

It's not just the information that you gather but the way in which you present it that determines whether people will read it or ignore it. By the way, this isn't purely from a parent/carer perspective or school perspective – we feel it's a real life lesson in general!

If you present it with a formal email that translates along the lines of 'I hereby announce that these are my child's needs – and I'm going to nail your sorry backside to the wall if you don't abide by them!' (Debby wrote that part, for the record!), then don't expect them to be exactly welcomed.

This is not a document to be used as evidence that the school is failing your child and shouldn't be introduced as such; opening up a collaborative approach is important and first impressions are essential...

You are presenting your classroom tips chart as helpful advice that will improve your child's chances at school, reduce disruption and act as a stitch in time for teachers who don't know them that well. In other words, it is there to make life easier, not harder.

So perhaps this would be a less daunting introduction to your notes:

Dear Mrs Bric-a-Brac...

I thought you might find the attached helpful when Jim joins in September. His teaching assistant, teacher and I have made notes on any daily difficulties and what worked successfully to combat them. I hope that his staff find it useful in getting to know him – if you could forward it to each of them, I'd be really grateful.

Look forward to meeting you in person!

TIPS

- Call the teacher by their name – and whatever you do, never address a letter or email with To Whom It May Concern, unless you feel that their bin is in urgent need of a paper meal. By the way, says Gareth, the same goes for schools when it comes to parents/carers: *never* use 'Mum', for example!

- Note the buoyant positive tone of the email, rather than 'An unexploded bomb is about to land in your school and you'd better be ready or I'll be holding you personally accountable'.

Another document that was provided for Bobby's staff (with the help of an excellent transition worker) was a visual escalation chart.

It was used to express what Bobby's body language looked like when he was starting to become agitated, shown on a rising scale from 1 (calm) to 5 (distressed). This was both for Bobby and teaching staff, so that they would have adequate warning that proactive intervention was needed in order to prevent an explosive moment. It was also a necessary step in Bobby being able to develop strategies independently and know more about himself. More about this in the next chapter.

STARTING A GOOD RELATIONSHIP

Something mentioned in Debby's 2018 book *Fifteen Things They Forgot to Tell You About Autism* is worth repeating here, and not just because Debby fancies more royalties (says Gareth!).

When talking about your child to new staff, think of the cocktail-party scenario.

You're at a cocktail party (humour us). We haven't met you before and someone brings you over to us. 'I don't believe you've met,' she says as she introduces you – and then proceeds to tell us all about your worst personality traits. OMG, you have so many...

Our smiles start to fade and one of us makes some excuse about needing to find another drink. The other one of us claims to have an urgent appointment tidying their sock drawer.

This is the equivalent of what some parents do when handing over their child for the first time to someone new. They list their child's 'disorders' and then issue a list of stark warnings to go alongside them.

It is understandable; the reasoning behind this is often 'Will you cope with the worst my child can throw at you?' You don't want them to get a nasty surprise, right?

The best results, however, come when someone *wants* to do a job. To start by knowing the most rewarding aspects of a task makes us more motivated. If we champion our kids and show everyone what we love about them, other carers form their initial impressions based on the upside and are more likely to respond better to the challenges.

Bobby did (and still does) have his challenges, but he was also kind, thoughtful, funny and insightful. These traits were talked about first; to start positive and *believe* positive is pretty important, we feel.

And while we're talking about first impressions, think about yourself, too. Consider your mood and demeanour when you first introduce yourself to new staff. This is a sales job. No, really – it is: from both school and family perspectives! The first impression that you create will determine whether you're viewed as a parent worth listening to or someone who is going to be a thorn in the school's side.

On the other side of the fence, how a school initially presents itself shows whether it will be a setting in which staff will listen and collaborate, or ignore and be inflexible.

If there are any problems, you want to be heard. That will be more likely to happen if you establish a positive rapport right from the start.

> *If there are any problems, you want to be heard. That will be more likely to happen if you establish a positive rapport right from the start.*

Rather than handing the school potential problems on a plate, as a carer you can suggest that you'd welcome thoughts on a few things that are worth the school knowing about early, adding that you have a few ideas of your own.

Reward good early communication by thanking them for it and reinforcing how much you're looking forward to working together.

Establish the idea that you're willing to develop solutions as a team, rather than take an adversarial stance when things go wrong.

CHAPTER 3

PREPARING THE GROUND FOR SECONDARY SCHOOL

Although getting used to a new physical environment is important for our children, what's equally important is that you prepare them for it emotionally.

The difficulty we face here is that, in emotional terms, many autistic children tend to go from nought to a hundred in under 40 seconds (or appear to, if we miss the signs of stress building over time).

A mind that's on red alert a lot of the time can't really cope with expressing in articulate terms why today isn't working for them. That's as important for your child to know as it is for you.

And therein lies our challenge when we prepare our kids for secondary school and their new secondary school prepares for them.

They need to be able to recognise and alert staff to difficulties early.

This will prevent the sorts of problems that require ten people sitting around a meeting table with a 'behaviour plan' in front of them, plus one rather bemused teenager who is being 'included' in this meeting for reasons that are a mystery to them. (Debby's painful observation there caused Gareth to say 'Argghhh!' and retreat to a quiet room to do some breathing exercises! He's seen too much of this kind of scenario.)

Parents, TAs and SENCos are great advocates, but the best champion for an autistic child is *themselves*.

So, two great skills in your child's secondary school toolkit include the ability to:

★ spot when things are getting too much for them and

★ express this calmly before they hit complete overload.

That's where you come in. Here's how carers can prepare a youngster to spot and report signs of anxiety:

1. ENSURE THEY ARE AWARE OF WHAT DRIVES OVERLOAD

This is very specific to them. If it's too noisy, what should they do? If they feel overloaded with jobs/tasks, what can they do to feel less anxious? Knowing ourselves is the key to recognising our likely triggers.

2. HELP THEM TO RECOGNISE THE LINK BETWEEN MIND AND BODY

When this young person is starting to get upset at home, what signals does their body give to them and how can you tell visibly that they are getting anxious? Do they start moving in an agitated way or twiddling hair, or do certain types of echolalia (repetition of familiar phrases) become very evident?

This sounds obvious, but, as Debby explains, her own son wasn't aware that stomach ache could be linked to stress. Plus, he wasn't really conscious that when he crossed his arms and started shaking his head, it was a sign that he was shifting up a gear emotionally.

Learning to recognise those signals is important; it means that your child knows when they need to engage 'calming strategy' mode.

You can help your youngster to notice the links between mind and body by pointing out your own experiences.

Wow, I'm excited about that, my body feels all tingly and I can't stand still!

Or:

You know earlier when I felt irritated – I could feel it because my arms felt all stiff and I was clamping my teeth together. Is that how you know if you are getting angry or is it different for you?

When they do start to get agitated, gently point it out:

When you start to move from side to side, that tells me that your thoughts are getting upsetting.

These strategies work well in school, too; talking about stressors and actively teaching calming/coping strategies is very powerful. Strategies that are deployed and developed across both home and school are far more effective than in one setting alone!

This field is called meta-cognition (a posh phrase that means 'thinking about thinking') and there are some fantastic books by Dawn Huebner and Dr Heather MacKenzie for autistic children aimed at helping them to recognise thoughts and feelings and to calm themselves – see Appendix 2: References and Resources, which are helpfully divided into each chapter for you to find the references easily.

3. INTRODUCE A VISUAL THERMOMETER

One great way of helping children to understand when their mood is escalating (and the thoughts linked to this) is to introduce them to a system that helps them to roughly rate the strength of their emotions in terms of a scale.

In primary school, a traffic light visual is nice and easy.

Pointing to green means they are okay and calm, orange means their feelings are starting to get too much, and I think you can guess what red is.

If you practise the traffic light system at home, then you're giving your child the practice they need to identify their own emotions and report them to someone when they're on 'orange'.

When they get older, it's possible to use a slightly more sophisticated scale.

Debby's son used *The Incredible 5-Point Scale* by Kari Dunn Buron and Mitzi Curtis. It's incredibly simple and effective. This brilliant book shows how adaptable a scale can be. It isn't just used for one thing, and it's well worth reading to see the range of strategies that the scale system can be used for.

The key here is to help your youngster to identify how they know when they are feeling calm and the relaxed signals their bodies give them. Then work with them to point out what happens in their mood, body and language as their emotions rise through the numbered scale. Colour-coding can be used to highlight each stage.

What is really important, however, is to actively teach the strategies to be used at each level, so that they know exactly what to do when their feelings start to get too much for them. The first strategy, of course, is to tell someone.

Bear in mind here that no strategy is a one-size-fits-all. It's important for adults not to impose a fixed, medicalised process on children, but instead to draw on certain tools that serve a purpose at that time and that age, which may change over time.

As with any system or tool, this is about how you implement it. If you want to use the thermometer method, tell school about it, encourage them to reinforce explanations of it (once isn't enough) and make sure that everyone knows about its presence. It's really important that staff shouldn't assume that your child knows how it works and will use it; reminders are key to the success of this sort of system, as Gareth can testify from using it in practice. These kinds of strategies most certainly aren't a case of 'Done! Move on!' (dusts hands, stress preparation sorted...). Careful consideration of these techniques as part of overall support is key.

One last thought from Gareth. Schools can have a habit of using 'off the shelf' strategies without much thought.

Stress thermometers should be personalised. It's not enough just to stick a colour chart in front of a young person with 'calm' and the bottom and 'meltdown' at the top. You might smile wryly when we write that, but this is all too common. Such strategies need to identify very specifically those thoughts and movements that are at each stage, and this is something that you as a parent or carer can help with.

Why do these visual systems work so well? Abstract ideas are hard for autistic people. These systems turn abstracts into a solid form. Colours and numbers give you a powerful common language to work with.

This also works from a teaching perspective. Not all signs of stress are easy to read. For instance, someone might use increasing echolalia (repeating phrases to themselves) if distressed. Unless you understand what a particular echolalia pattern means, it could be hard to interpret. Someone might use certain phrases when they're happy, and another type when they aren't.

So as well as creating a visual thermometer for your child, you can provide a separate copy for teachers with extra notes on what you do at home at each level of the scale to diffuse anxiety.

Outbursts are pretty easy to spot, the early warning signs less so. Plus some kids don't have outbursts when overloaded; they go into a form of shutdown instead. So warning signals can be very useful.

If you have a child who closes off when upset or anxious, it's important to make staff aware, but also to ask them to build in times for check-ins when things are calm, so that they don't end up having to react to a 'shutdown' when things have gone wrong.

> **TIP**
> Don't assume that the school will know what your child's stress-ors are. For instance, loud public praise and congratulations for some autistic children can be so overwhelming as to lead to overload. If this is the case, as we always say, tell them – forewarned is forearmed!

4. TUNE IN YOUR COMMUNICATION CHANNELS

Parents, we know that you expect to be your child's advocate – that's why you've been diligent enough to pick up this book.

For that reason, it's best to ensure that you have a great dialogue with your child at home. The parents we know who have been most successful in helping their children have fostered a great atmosphere of openness.

So how do you create a great dialogue ready for 'big' school?

You may have an evening routine already with a bedtime story. This sometimes lasts longer with autistic kids. (Here, Debby painfully rec-ollects that after reading the same Horrid Henry story approximately 4300 times, she had to tell her son she could take no more.)

As children reach secondary age, there's a risk that in losing the bed-time story slot, you also lose a valuable communication opportunity.

Instead, keep the same slot, but turn it into 'chat time'.

As your child grows into a tween, keep the bedtime story slot, but turn it into chat time.

Chat time is a calm time in the evening after the wind-down from school and bath or shower, when they can express whatever they want to about their day.

If they want to spend ten minutes talking about Minecraft, Nintendo, unicorns, dinosaurs, buses or time travel, so be it. They lead the chat; you follow.

This isn't the time to ask earnest questions about their mental wellbeing (tempting as this might be); you're simply available and listening. They don't have to process queries, just enjoy your company.

This time is child-led; avoid firing lots of questions – let them decide what to chat about. Try not to assume what their difficulties might be; keeping an open mind is important. By the way, don't call it 'chat time'. Just show up to keep them company.

If they say they don't want to talk and ask you to leave, respect that, but still show up every evening.

This dedicated time will maintain good bonds, so that if things do start to get stressful, you've already got a channel tuned in and are ready to pick up signals.

Whatever you do, don't be tempted to have a chat that ends with 'By the way this room looks a state and have you done your homework?'

The experience has to be positive every single time in order to work. For that time in the evening, you're in buddy mode. This is so important as our kids get to secondary age; they are still vulnerable and yet prone to closing off as teenagers do.

Also use the evening as an opportunity to talk through any plans for the following day, noting reminders on a wipe-off board or printing out a schedule if this visual will settle the mind.

Knowing that important reminders won't 'escape' from your brain because they are written down is a useful sleep aid for anyone!

5. ADDRESS THE TENDENCY TO CATASTROPHISE

Tim was a volunteer at *AuKids* magazine, which Debby co-founded. As an autistic adult, he was tenacious and resourceful. But if something negative happened to him, he became overcome quite quickly.

From Debby's personal experience and that of her readers, Debby knew that Tim wasn't alone. Catastrophising can be one of the unwanted side effects of rigid thinking, of thought processes that tend to jump between black and white.

Debby and her co-editor Tori bought Tim a diary, and along with it they purchased large stickers showing happy, sad and neutral faces. The happy faces were all yellow, the sad were all blue and the neutral faces were green.

Tim has trouble expressing his feelings, so they asked him to use a sticker to report on each morning and afternoon, and to make notes if he wanted to by the side of each sticker.

They called this his Mood Diary.

Tim's mood diary changed his responses to the week in a dramatic way.

The next week, he arrived beaming. When he'd put a happy face in his diary and wrote that he'd met a friend, staring at it caused him to absorb great feelings.

It had also given him solid evidence of his week, which helped him to gain perspective and to avoid catastrophising.

If he'd had one bad moment at work, it was confined to one afternoon. The amount of happy and neutral faces told their own story. Rather than that one moment taking over his thoughts about the entire week, he was able to balance his thoughts visually.

Perhaps this could be something you'd like to try, too?

6. PLAN THE BACK-UP!

So we know how to check in with our feelings and we understand them a little better. And now on to the back-up plan.

It's helpful if a child understands who to turn to and when if they have a difficulty at school.

Make sure that both you and your child know the right people to approach with various different difficulties. Ensure that they are clear what their TA is there for (it's not that obvious!), what questions they need to reserve for the class teacher, the form tutor, the head of year and any other support staff. Also, what can they ask other pupils, or a buddy, about?

Jointly producing a simple document with pictures of key staff can be useful to have as a reminder to refer to throughout the day, as required.

Gareth recommends that school staff regularly check a child's understanding of this information and avoid purely verbal instructions, which is why a physical sheet in the pocket can be handy.

As with most things autism-related, it's not enough to assume that an autistic youngster knows exactly how to tackle a difficulty. Showing them a definite pathway will give them control, which in turn will reduce what we call 'background anxiety', the sort of constant anxiety that leads to overload.

Calm, consistent, proactive planning is powerful!

TIP FOR SCHOOLS

It's important not to make assumptions. This means actively teaching a youngster how to go to a particular person and checking to see if they are able to. Do they know where they are located, how to find them and what to do if they are unavailable?

WHAT THE SCHOOL CAN DO...

At Gareth's school, the Curriculum Support team developed an A4 single-sided 'student passport' for each pupil who benefitted from it (irrespective of a diagnosis or label), in collaboration with the pupil themselves.

A STUDENT PASSPORT CONTAINS

- student information and photograph
- 'I would like you to know that...' (the young person's first-hand description)

- 'This means that...' (again 'first-hand' information for teachers from the student)
- 'I find it difficult to...' (key areas that are difficult, agreed after discussion)
- 'It would help me if you could...' (practical strategies and tips to support the identified areas)
- 'I will help myself by...' (agreed strategies and practical solutions for the young person)
- additional support (noted additional support, SALT therapy sessions, TA support, etc.)
- data/information (key data, information as required – summaries for ease of reference).

Each teacher was given a copy and had it readily available for classes. It provided an at-a-glance guide as they got to know each pupil, and was something that could be quickly and easily updated.

You can find information on creating a student passport in Appendix 2: References and Resources, including a film clip of Gareth talking about the principles behind them; there's also a template of one in Appendix 1: Useful Charts.

CHAPTER 4

BUILDING THE FOUNDATIONS FOR COLLABORATION

Sadly, we're certain that many parents and carers reading this book will have faced, or be facing, a potential conflict with education staff.

Around 90% of the e-mails Debby received at *AuKids* magazine were from carers wanting to know how to deal with schools that didn't seem to 'get' autism.

However, if knowledge and information can be passed between school and home in the right way, trust can be built on both sides and maybe we can prevent some of these conflicts from arising.

Good collaboration is about the relocation of power, not the school trying to impose dominance over families. This isn't a sign of weakness but of great strength.

At times, you'll find that even with the best approaches, education staff either won't accept your explanations or don't have sufficient expertise to apply the right solutions. In these cases, it's a good idea to ask for impartial help and advice from outside experts. We'll be looking at this in more detail in Chapter 13.

Trust, however, is something that both sides can easily work to achieve right from the start, and it is within everyone's gift to build it, develop it and learn from each other.

As a starting point, we're going to look into how a trusting relationship can be built between school and home – a sound basis for collaboration that will give your knowledge and information the best chance of being absorbed.

You'll find that in this book, we repeatedly adopt the mantra 'prevention is better than cure; be more proactive and less reactive'.

Good collaboration is central to building trust. So we're going to start with the question of how parents and teachers can become a highly effective collaborative team.

Although we'll be talking about conflict resolution in Chapters 11 and 12, our focus right here is trying to establish the kind of communication that makes you less likely to reach a point of conflict.

More proactive, less reactive! Always!

Disagreements can – and will – still happen, but let's give you a good chance of having a great relationship in the first place. That way, despite disagreements, you'll be more able to work together.

Our experience is that starting from a positive place means disagreements can be civil and open; too often, mistrust means disagreements are heated and bitter. Getting that solid foundation to start with is vital.

If you're a carer reading this, you might ask yourself why you're being asked to think so carefully about tactfully building a relationship with school staff. Shouldn't they just get on and listen without you having to think about your messages? Isn't it their job to have your child's best interests at heart? Why should it be down to you to manage feelings and responses?

And if you're a teacher reading this, you might think, 'Shouldn't they just listen to me? I know what I'm doing. This is my job. Why should I be thinking about persuasion or collaboration?'

If you're a parent reading this, the answer is that different people have different views on how to solve difficulties at school, and if you're explaining to a teacher that their career-defining approach needs to be tweaked for the sake of *your* child, you need to be sure that you do this in a way that respects someone else's reality, even if their judgement is slightly askew right now.

And if you're a teacher reading this, the answer is that you're the education expert, but carers are the experts in their own children. Without working closely together, you may miss a piece of information that proves vital to problem-solving. Working closely also means you get the best of both areas of expertise – surely a win-win?

In our view, there is no situation that won't benefit from carers and teachers building a good understanding early on.

This is how effective provision works; collaboration and honesty is fundamental for good outcomes and was most certainly so from Debby and Gareth's experience.

SHARE INFORMATION EARLY

From the parent/carer side, the first step is to give the school all the information it needs to establish an in-depth understanding of your child right from the get-go. This was mentioned earlier in the book, when we wrote about the classroom tips chart that you can collate during the final years at primary school.

Forewarned is forearmed, as we've said, and knowing in advance allows for better planning and – you guessed it – proactive working. The beauty of those notes is that they can detail certain 'triggers' (not our favourite term) and reasons for them. Nope, it was there in black and white: as sure as eggs is eggs, if you set off a fire alarm without warning, he *will* be distressed and may well hit someone as a result of being dysregulated from the unexpected sensory overload.

MEET FACE TO FACE

A key step for parents and carers is to meet staff face to face as early in your child's secondary school career as possible. Meeting individual subject tutors may not be possible until arranged parents' evenings, but you should certainly make it a priority to meet your child's SENCo and form tutor in person. If your child has a subject that is pivotal to their success in life because it's their passion, do ask to chat to that teacher too (at the very least, get their email address).

If your school is on the ball, contact information will be supplied in advance for you. If not, create yourself a go-to sheet with images of the key staff and their names, roles, email addresses and phone numbers.

Why is meeting in person so important?

Emailing a member of staff when you've never met them personally is very much like disagreeing with another driver through gestures and a closed car window! You've no idea what they're like as an individual, the context for their decisions or the reason for them. Written exchanges can take a stilted and impersonal tone – in fact, you may as well be talking to a computer. Go see them, tell them that you're worried or anxious and why. Don't just take it out on the keyboard. More about that later.

Emailing a member of staff when you've never met them personally is very much like disagreeing with another driver through gestures and a closed car window!

Meeting in person at school, you can establish a positive basis from which to work. If you're a parent, let school know that they should consider you part of their team and that you're happy to share knowledge that may be helpful at any point. The 'here to help' message should be loud and clear. This openness and warmth helps to ease any feelings of fear over a lack of autism knowledge.

ASK FOR OPENNESS AND HONESTY

If you openly state that some characteristics of a child may be a bit confusing and you're happy to help interpret them, then you've advanced one step with communication. You're saying that you don't expect perfect autism knowledge, but that you would welcome great communication and a solid base from which to develop the specific knowledge for your child. Personalisation is essential in the long run.

If we're comparing this relationship to building a tent, the first post is now in – you've already found the best pitch after choosing this school!

If there's any confusion over how to support your child, or something is interfering with their learning, the school should feel relaxed about contacting you to find out more, even if this isn't yet a particular issue.

By saying this, you're encouraging an open dialogue and for the school to acknowledge potential issues early and avoid sweeping problems under the carpet, rather than feel as if school shouldn't bother you unless something has become a major stumbling block. This can lead to issues being stored up for the future.

You may feel that you are a very busy person and you don't want to be on call for your child's school. Believe us, though, the odd small email or discussion as early clarification will save you a lot of time in the long run if you can keep positive and open in your manner.

This isn't just about nipping problems in the bud. This is nipping them before they even *think* about being a bud! Go on, you know what is coming... Be proactive – let's just leave that there!

PREDICT STUMBLING BLOCKS

We've often found that home–school diaries, often gold dust during the junior years, have been abruptly halted in secondary school.

In the absence of a home–school diary, it does help to encourage independence by teaching your child to make a note of what they need to plan for.

However, planning and short-term memory can be affected in autism (and amplified further in an autistic *teenager*!), so it's good to have a note yourself, so that you can check they have remembered and step in if they haven't.

We will be mentioning this again later when we talk about 'trip-wire practices' in Chapters 6 and 7 on jumping barriers.

If there isn't a daily communication method, ask the TA to let you know directly in advance if:

★ there is something you need to pay for

★ there are forms to fill in that have been left in your child's bag or are digital in nature

★ an inset day is coming up

★ a non-uniform day is coming up.

You can then support your child in updating their calendars and diaries, and nothing will create a last-minute panic. If school is proactive in doing this as well, a 'safety net' approach is established. This won't eliminate all potential challenges but most certainly will reduce them.

When your teenager gets home, a wipe-off board in their room can prompt them with tomorrow's plan, if anything extra is needed.

Laminating your own planning boards for home and including special interest images make them more fun. (Laminators are inexpensive and needn't take up much room.)

SHOW CONFIDENCE AND TRUST

It's natural to feel trepidation as your child starts secondary school, but try to show that you have trust and confidence in staff and are looking forward to working with them. This establishes a positive impression of you as someone who will be a pleasure to work with.

Why is this so important? Staff are far more likely to initiate an informal chat if you sound easy-going than if you've seemed negative on their first meeting with you. Trust us, we know how hard this can be, especially if past experiences have left you angry and disillusioned. But it's still important.

So you've left them with a positive impression and you've got to know them face to face. Good start.

CATCH THEM DOING IT RIGHT!

The next stage is to keep in contact with staff *when nothing upsetting is happening.* Yes, it's in italics. We're emphasising, not shouting.

If you were the boss managing a team, and you only ever spoke to them when there was something to criticise, the chances are you'd not have a very motivated team. The same psychology works here.

If the school does something well and it suits your child, get in touch straight away and thank them. A quick email is great. Tell them what they did right and why! As we're fond of saying, there's nothing in the word 'no' that tells you what you should be doing instead. Catch people doing things right, and they know what to repeat.

> There's nothing in the word 'no' that tells a school what it should be doing instead.

Although Debby's parental radar is actively scanning for problems, it's also highly attuned to signals that things are working.

So, when the school listens to your views, show real appreciation:

Thanks for that productive conversation.

I really appreciated sharing my views with you.

Hope that these ideas will be helpful.

Thanks for working so closely with me.

The last email Debby wrote was offering help and support to new staff who didn't know her son well at college, and making some suggestions about how some things could be made easier in class.

As a result, one of the staff moved Bobby to a quieter position in the room. Debby made it clear in a thank-you email that she was appreciative of his thoughtfulness and flexibility. The message is 'I am someone you can work with and I notice the effort that you're making'.

The way that you write these little messages will be the difference between looking like a busybody parent who is dedicated to the fine art of micro-managing and being regarded as a helpful and useful member of the team who will diminish stress at work rather than add to it. So...

USE POSITIVE LANGUAGE

Thinking about what you say and the tone in which you say it will reap rewards in your development of positive relationships, whether that's with education staff or in any other working partnerships.

If you want the best chance of being listened to, use words that energise rather than words that drain.

Words that drain include phrases such as:

It really upsets him when...

I feel strongly that you shouldn't...

Please could you make sure...

If you're absolutely desperate that your advice is heeded, and in particular if you've had bad experiences in the past, you could slip into that draining form of communication extremely easily.

Like it or not, people will be more likely to heed your advice if there's something in it for *them*. Show them how you are making life easier for them.

Words that energise include phrases like:

I've found he's really receptive if you...
Here's something I've found that I think you might find really helpful...
If you don't mind me sharing a personal experience here...

Flip your suggestion on its head so instead of what they *shouldn't* do, you are sharing what *works* instead.

This automatically means that you're searching those autism folders in your mind for an answer to a problem rather than just complaining about something that's wrong, so it automatically makes you solution-focused. We cannot emphasise this enough.

You aren't just being nice for the sake of it; you're investing in your own peace of mind by building a great relationship.

OWN THE PROBLEM-SOLVING

Supposing you don't really have an answer? If you take the attitude that 'school will sort it', school might sort it in a way you don't much like. The constructive suggestion is to offer to work together to find a solution:

Christopher has been feeling overwhelmed during chemistry classes and to be honest, without more information, I'm not sure how I can help you to get to the bottom of this. Shall we meet up for a quick chat?

In other words, write yourself into the story as someone who is part of the solution, not just someone they report to when they've already implemented it.

TREAT THEM WITH RESPECT

The last step is to remember to be respectful of your team.

You may be in a hurry in the morning, but if you've had a rush and an upset child bordering on 'meltdown', handing them over without explanation is a bit like chucking a lit match into a firework factory.

A quick call, email, phone call, text, carrier pigeon, whatever, to say that this is a day to reduce demands, as unfortunately you had a bad start, is really helpful information and will be appreciated.

CHAPTER 5

COMFORT AMONG THE COMMOTION

One of the ways of reducing the chance of a crisis at school is to talk to your setting about how to keep your youngster's environment nice and calming for them. 'Background calm' (as we call it) acts as a shield protecting children from additional anxiety and enabling them to cope with pressures more easily.

So, as well as building the foundations for your relationship with school, let's ensure that 'background calm' provides a solid foundation for the classroom, too – and beyond.

The charity Fixers, which received the Queen's Award for Voluntary Service, is a campaigning organisation dedicated to change, helping young people to 'fix' the future by sharing their past experiences. Their work continues to be influential.

In 2018, they produced a report sharing the views of autistic young people who called for changes to help them achieve better results in the classroom.

This report – 'Feel Happy on the Spectrum' – gave a voice to autistic contributors (most of them in their early 20s with secondary school a very recent memory) who recommended improved peer understanding of autism in schools. Coincidentally, this is a key element of the Saturation Model, which you'll read about in Chapter 8.

Fixers also underlined the need for more focus on classroom-based assessment of support, rather than purely an emphasis on autism as a diagnosis.

We'll get to peer understanding in time, but in this chapter we'd like to slightly redefine what is understood by 'support'.

Most people understand classroom support to mean breaking tasks into smaller chunks, adapting work to make it more accessible or using planning 'scaffolding' to help support autistic pupils to systematically make their way through a piece of work. These are all highly relevant – and we will be writing about them in Chapters 6 and 7.

However, we also want to focus on what we feel is being missed. For autistic pupils, background calm is the starting point of all productive learning.

BACKGROUND CALM – THE ENVIRONMENT

If you're a parent or carer, be proactive when it comes to communicating the challenges around the school day. Identify what they are likely to be and discuss solutions early. You don't have to wait for an unpleasant experience to happen; you may be perfectly aware that your child finds a large, echoing canteen or sports hall overwhelming. What can be done?

Again, this is where note-taking in the last few years of primary school can be really handy. You'll be able to identify environments and situations that are likely to cause distress, and they can be predicted and prevented at secondary school.

WHAT CAN SCHOOLS DO?

When training schools in inclusive practices, Gareth talks about the idea of 'constant consistency'.

This is about ensuring that pockets of 'good practice' are not undone by inconsistent whole-school provision and systems.

It isn't any good having a really calm, consistent, purposeful learning environment in one classroom, if, when the bell goes for break or lunch, there's a stampede down the corridor.

This just adds significant stress for students who find these less structured times extremely challenging.

The answer is ensuring a clear link between policy and practice, another key area of the Saturation Model – be patient and you'll read all about it!

Creating a seamless, positive experience from classroom to classroom and in all areas in between is the key to unlocking success for everyone. No one is harmed by calm, consistent, positive approaches, whereas many can experience significant distress from noisy, hectic and dysregulated ones.

Whole-school policies that promote 'constant consistency' include:

★ getting rid of bells

★ promoting orderly transitions (staggering timings for some students)

★ staff eating lunch with students.

The key for any school is listening to the voices of young people and their families, finding out what is challenging for them and designing solutions together.

It won't surprise you to learn that one mistake Gareth often identifies in mainstream schools is environments that only allow for reactive rather than proactive strategies.

This means that assumptions are made about what's needed, rather than taking a really in-depth look at what's required using a family's past experiences with each young person as a starting point. More about 'constant consistency' for schools in Chapter 8.

CREATE A STRESS SUPPORT PLAN

Most difficulties at mainstream school can be pre-empted simply by noting causes of stress and predicting when they are likely to happen. So, jointly identify stressors and note what is being done to reduce them. A plan also includes appropriate coping strategies (and explicitly explaining how to use them). The key to this approach, says Gareth, is that it forms part of a 'philosophy of care', and rather than being a tick-box exercise or a formatted form, it is tailor-made for each student who needs one and is used to help teachers better understand their students.

PIVOTAL COMFORTS IN CLASS

What's often overlooked in terms of classroom support for autistic pupils is an appreciation of the small comforts that help them to self-regulate, either in an emotional or a sensory way. We call them 'pivotal comforts'.

Appreciating them means being flexible and tolerant around their use, rather than seeing them as unnecessary, unfair on others or distracting.

> *Appreciating pivotal comforts means being flexible and tolerant around their use, rather than seeing them as unnecessary, unfair on others or distracting.*

Autistic kids know what works for them; in an overwhelming world, they've spent their early childhood searching for things that help them to maintain a sense of calm.

In her wonderful book *But you don't look autistic at all*, Bianca Toeps underlines this point:

> The limitations in communication and social interaction are listed at the top (of diagnostic criteria) because those are what an outsider notices first... But if you ask autistic people what they struggle with most, it's usually overstimulation they mention first.

So when we think about classroom support, let's think about how autism feels on the inside rather than how it looks to others.

As the American poet Robert Frost is quoted as saying: 'Don't ever take a fence down until you know why it has been put up.'

Far from being irrelevant or an afterthought, comforting items help autistic children to combat an overwhelming environment and to regulate that all too easily triggered fight-or-flight system.

When we tried to look up quotes relating to comfort in a working environment, we found many implying distraction and laziness. It's not hard to see why comfort items are traditionally viewed as mere distractions or inappropriate for secondary aged children.

In fact, when you think about it, even the phrase 'comfort zone' carries negative connotations of staying safe and not exploring new areas.

However, rather than being a hindrance, keeping inside their comfort zones is actually rather important, helping autistic kids to realise their potential, to innovate and to work productively.

Autistic people are often working in a state of high anxiety because of constant processing of unfamiliar information plus environmental overload. Comfort is vital in reducing that sense of overload. It is highly underestimated in secondary schools which, as mentioned before, are possibly some of the least comforting environments to be in!

When a child at school has an outburst, this isn't generally a response to one huge demand or one emotional incident. More often, it's the accumulation of many smaller demands throughout the day, and this is why it's important to minimise the impact of those demands. Funnily enough most moments of dysregulation are preceded by requests; simply reducing these can have a direct impact on such moments, almost immediately.

However, daily comforts can also shield children from that impact by calming their anxiety responses and preventing tension from building up.

Debby knows how important their *stuff* is to autistic kids, partly through her own experience and partly because she constantly has parents telling her about it!

One parent said: 'My daughter will not go to school without her toy dog. They aren't particularly keen on her having him there but they know that she wouldn't cope without him.'

As Dr Luke Beardon writes:

> We cannot change all the things that make a child feel unsafe, though we should do everything we can – but what we can do is work out ways of identifying aspects of life where the child does feel safe... I have witnessed first-hand examples of schools taking items that are a source of comfort off children using 'age-inappropriateness' as a rationale. It is not a valid rationale. Absolutely encourage keeping items that make your child feel secure, but do so in ways that will keep the child safe from being teased or bullied...
>
> *Extract from* Avoiding Anxiety in Autistic Children
> *by Luke Beardon (2020), reproduced by permission of*
> *Sheldon Press, an imprint of John Murray Press*

One dad wrote to us to say: 'Ned is in adult education now, but he has always taken loads of stuff with him everywhere he goes. He still packs a 150 litre sports bag for 48 hours of respite (no, that's not a typo).'

You may find that as the stresses at school get higher, a backpack becomes bigger. It's a signal that the young person needs security.

Before Debby's son Bobby joined secondary school, she remembers reading a list of new school rules with some trepidation. No personal items were allowed to be taken into school, particularly electronic devices.

Gulp.

If Bobby didn't have his Nintendo 3DS with him, the sky would surely cave in. Bobby's toy Pikachu accompanied him everywhere. It was unthinkable to ask him to give those things up just when he needed them most.

Fortunately, Debby communicated these concerns to Bobby's outreach worker. Not a problem – the Nintendo 3DS could be kept in his locker, and Pikachu wasn't an issue. After all, as we mentioned before, making reasonable adjustments was a key area in Gareth and Debby's working partnership. Those rules were easily adapted to accommodate SEN pupils. In fact, Pikachu became the classroom mascot and appeared in his class photograph (his grandma knitted it a school tie, although Bobby insisted this wasn't an appropriate dress code for a Pokémon).

But what should you do if your school is not as understanding? Margaret, a parent, writes:

My son used to love taking Blu Tack™ to school. At primary school it was occasionally used as a punishment – 'You can't have your Blu Tack™ until you do this piece of work!' All the 'punishment' did was make him cry and the work never got done!

Actually, although Margaret's son appeared as if he was not paying attention when fiddling with Blu Tack™, he was listening fully.

She added:

I think the point really is that it irritates some teachers if they see a child fiddling with something, or not looking at them, and interpret that as the child is distracted and therefore not paying attention, but for some children the only way to be able to pay attention is to have their 'pivotal comfort' and as my husband pointed out – fiddling with the Blu Tack™ helped him to pay attention and he would have been more distracted without it.

We wouldn't remove a wheelchair or hearing aid from a student, yet we often deny young people their own coping mechanisms through the unintended consequences of wider systems and policies, as Gareth often states when delivering training and explaining this concept further.

> We wouldn't remove a wheelchair or hearing aid from a student, yet we often deny young people their own coping mechanisms through unintended consequences of wider systems and policies.

Those things that autistic pupils use to regulate themselves are non-negotiable. They can't be used as a bargaining chip.

Margaret's son did find a way around the problem. 'He was given a small smooth olive wood cross one Easter and I noticed after he stopped the Blu Tack™, he kept the cross hidden and would sometimes just stroke it if he was feeling stressed, but it never came out of his pocket!'

Even when staff understood about the Blu Tack™, peers didn't.

Fellow students weren't understanding and it drew unwanted attention which he hated so he stopped taking it in. I don't think the other students were being unkind, but intrigued (maybe even impressed at the fantastic model creations he made) and asking questions, but he has social anxiety and couldn't cope with the attention.

This is another reason why peer education is essential as part of an inclusive approach.

Part of the reason why these 'pivotal comforts' are overlooked is a lack of understanding as to why they are so vital.

Some schools feel that in order to encourage independence these props should be banned. But if you recognise self-regulation as a key area in autism that causes difficulties in school, then it follows that you should welcome anything that aids self-regulation, providing it causes no harm.

So what should you do to help school recognise the necessity of these comforts?

IDENTIFY WHAT THEY ARE

First things first. You can do something really positive for an autistic child by clearly identifying what their 'pivotal comforts' are.

Pivotal comforts aren't only *things*, but breathing spaces – places of calm and quiet. It could be time to block chaotic thoughts by focusing on a computer game – generally frowned upon, but actually a very good 'reset' button for many autistic kids.

As well as having a quiet place to retreat to with his own desk as part of his personalised timetable, Debby's son Bobby was allowed computer time at breaks and lunchtime.

Unstructured social time can often be the most challenging for autistic pupils, and it's important that they have access to indoor places to go where they can spend some time on their own if they choose to. After taking in lots of verbal information and processing it all morning, autistic batteries need to recharge. The last thing they need is more input, unless it's in the form of a special interest, which recharges them.

Timetabled into Bobby's school day was also 20 minutes for him to use his meditation app (Headspace – www.headspace.com) – another chance to reset the brain after much processing work.

Again, this was identified by Debby as being one of his pivotal comforts. His TA then took this information and thought about how she could translate it into the timetable without any disruption to Bobby's education.

HAVE THEM MENTIONED IN PAPERWORK

For parents, we have a key piece of advice. Mentioning these comforts isn't a case of 'Oh and by the way...' Make them part of early conversations about helping emotional wellbeing and self-regulation, mention them to all staff and ensure that they are included in an EHCP if your child has one.

In other words, promote them to the top of the league!

According to the law, 'reasonable adjustments' must be made within the classroom for SEN pupils, but what exactly defines a reasonable adjustment? If we were to be precise, pivotal comforts would be on our list. School should measure the adjustment's impact on a person's learning and wellbeing against any genuine impact on others in the class.

A 'reasonable adjustment' in the case of an autistic pupil is letting them have those things around them that help them to regulate and therefore should be mentioned in the child's support notes.

EXPLAIN WHY

Again, as we mentioned, how you present these things to staff will probably influence whether or not you're ignored.

'He must have his comfort blanket; otherwise he'll get very upset!' might give the impression you're an over-anxious parent and that you are babying your child. Teachers who aren't as well versed in autism (and that particular child) as they should be may well look heaven-wards and think: 'This kid needs to grow up!' (which is obviously a very poor and uneducated viewpoint, but one Debby has heard too often).

Explain the comfort in terms of how it helps your child to self-reg-ulate and calm. How about:

> I've found it calms and focuses him to have comforts around him, because it aids his self-regulation, which is an issue for autistic people. So even if it's just in his bag, having his blanket visible will really help him.

Or:

> Just having pictures of his hobbies available to look at instantly calms his brain and allows him to focus.

PEER TRAINING

In denying pivotal comforts, some schools use the sentiment 'Other pupils won't think it's fair and won't understand'.

This is a bit of a weedy excuse, to phrase it charitably.

Peer training and education is essential – and the nature of it has to be meaningful and relate to what children are witnessing in the classroom. Why do autistic children need those things around them, and what extra strains are they facing in the classroom that are a threat to their nervous systems?

By giving adequate peer training, including an explanation of how the demands of an environment can overload an autistic person, schools can ensure that other pupils won't need to ask constant questions, singling out one individual for unwanted attention.

By the way, Debby speaks from personal experience. Because of great peer awareness training, Bobby was never teased about his Pikachu toy and other pupils knew it was too important to steal from him. It was simply 'part of Bobby' and that was that.

TAKING A LEAF OUT OF HOME EDUCATION'S BOOK...

Just before Bobby left, his school was also opening a new comfort lounge for any pupil who had mental health challenges. It was designed to feel like home and had beanbags, sensory lighting and other creature comforts.

In Hulme Hall Grammar School in Stockport, pupils and parents put together 'Happy Bags' that include photos and other calming items which help promote good feelings. They are left in a wellbeing room for when the pupil needs a break. The school also encourages use of mindfulness packs, including pens and colouring.

School is a demanding and, at times, impersonal environment. We have to learn lessons from home education families as to why their option is being increasingly chosen. It brings flexibility and creature comforts into the classroom, and we need to learn that lesson.

When it comes to an environment that is free from excessive stress, there is far more to consider than just noise, lighting and crowds.

TIPS

- **Pocket reminders:** If the thought of a particular situation causes anxiety, discuss three key things that could be done in that situation. Write key thoughts down on a piece of paper with your child. Show them that it's there in their pocket if needed. Even if it's not used, the fact that key advice is readily available will have a calming effect.

- **Colour-coded requests:** Some children don't like anything that draws attention to them in class and struggle to ask for support, but you could agree a subtle colour-coded system for use at school, so that your youngster could ask for help simply by putting a red card on their desk.

- **Virtual hugs:** Debby's son used to carry a 'hug' key, a small ornamental key that represented a 'hug from home', which he could touch if he needed reassurance. It just sat in his blazer pocket. (Gareth didn't even know this until Debby wrote it for the book – a truly effective personalised strategy that was just that, a personal thing.)

- **Comforting images:** Some comforting images of a special interest could work equally as well. Autistic adults report just how powerful even staring at an image can be. Tim likes to look at old postcards. 'When I stare at them, I feel as if I become part of the scene and it kind of floods my brain with happiness. It pushes to the side any negative thoughts. It's the same with my bus magazines. It's not just that I like them, the feeling of looking at them is more powerful than just that.'

CHAPTER 6

JUMPING THE BARRIERS: THE FIRST SIX

With autistic pupils, much of what we are used to identifying as a difficulty simply comes about as a result of an imbalance between the challenges faced and the coping resources to handle them. As Dodge and colleagues wrote in their paper 'The challenge of defining wellbeing':

> Stable wellbeing is when individuals have the psychological, social and physical resources they need to meet a particular psychological, social and/or physical challenge. When individuals have more challenges

than resources, the see-saw dips, along with their wellbeing, and vice-versa. (Dodge *et al.* 2012)

How can we as parents and carers help our children to do well in mainstream settings, knowing that these establishments present a range of very real hurdles that challenge our children's wellbeing?

There are three ways in which we can be effective:

1. Identify what is at the heart of each challenge, and make school aware of this if they aren't, so that effective practical adaptations can be made *before* problems arise.

2. Suggest helpful strategies to school that have worked successfully in the past or elsewhere. Share ideas and information with them.

3. Use strategies at home to help your child to develop a toolkit of resources, manage their stress levels and improve their ability to self-regulate.

In this chapter and the next, we're going to show you just some examples of how autism can influence how children learn and respond at school and how you can help to get the best for them.

In doing so, we hope to arm you with enough information to share with school in case your child's needs are misinterpreted. Since this is a large topic, we'll tackle six barriers in each of the two chapters.

A small disclaimer at this point: these aren't the only barriers within a learning environment by any means but are intended as a 'starter for ten', as it were.

We've only scratched the surface when it comes to sensory issues, for example, which may be hugely challenging for some children. If your child has difficulty reading facial expressions and connecting them with context (especially as expressions don't always reflect true inner feelings!), this social barrier can also affect their comprehension.

The key to these chapters is to help you start to identify the key factors for your own child that are likely to get in their way, and what can be done about them.

Barriers aren't purely obstacles at the time they happen. For instance, a flickering overhead light in the classroom won't just be distracting when the child is sitting underneath it. The thought of the flickering light – and having to endure it – will influence learning outside of that one classroom, both beforehand and afterwards.

This is why Gareth's notion of 'constant consistency' is so very crucial. One aspect of school life influences another, and it's only when all features of a setting work in harmony that an inclusive system really works.

As a parent or carer, the best you can do is predict potential triggers for stress, or obstacles, point them out and share possible solutions.

It is the SENCo's job to respond to these predictions and maybe identify some that those not familiar with the school wouldn't have anticipated.

It's also worth underlining that your child's involvement in these discussions, both with you and with the school itself, is absolutely essential. They know what works for them and it's helpful for development of self-expression if they can start to communicate it.

If pupils are at the heart of decision-making, it will not only build their confidence in the solutions being decided, but also help them to understand the entire process of negotiating adaptations.

As parents and carers, we're so used to sorting things out on behalf of our children that it can be quite a jump to have them attend and participate in meetings, but it's essential for their development. Then, as they grow older, they can start to manage their own environments by asking for adjustments, for quiet space...or whatever it is they need in order to be productive.

This is an important part of educating them in what it means to be an autistic person functioning well within a society in which non-autistic people are most commonly catered for.

So...let's have a go at prediction. How likely are the following barriers to affect your youngster? Do some of them affect them less than others? Or some of them, not at all? Once we've identified each barrier, we'll discuss how you can nip problems in the bud (our new favourite phrase).

COMMON BARRIERS

1. Lack of experience in 'framing' new events

Most of us have brains like filing cabinets. If we hit an unfamiliar situation, we mentally flick through our filing cabinets to see if there's anything near enough that can give us a helpful context.

In general, the information from several mental 'filing cabinets' is compiled and the brain responds: 'I see. I've got a reasonable idea of what to do now.'

This happens in milliseconds.

Autistic people do have mental filing cabinets – lots of them. They aren't lacking. What they may not have, however, is a person in the brain's virtual 'admin department' who can flick through all of them and compile a relevant report! Making sense of disparate experiences can be problematic.

In his essential read, *Autism as Context Blindness*, this is what Peter Vermeulen refers to as 'context blindness'. Every situation appears new and previous experience may not be of great value unless it's identical. In addition, secondary school pupils lack the life experience to 'frame' new situations. Older autistic people tend to cope much better simply because they can predict their own responses and have learnt what works for them.

In addition to this, difficulty self-regulating with autism (managing our own emotions and the way our bodies respond to them) can mean that a teen can find themselves in crisis when faced with a new experience.

What can we do?

a. Rate experiences

One useful exercise is to ask your teenager to rate how good or bad they feel a new experience is going to be – marks out of ten. After the experience, ask them to rate again how good or bad the experience *really was*. Keep these scores. They help to give your child evidence that new situations tend to turn out better than imagined.

b. Prepare your child

Preparation for new situations is *so* important. You can do much good by pre-empting even slight changes with specific information and visuals. In particular, focus on the world as they see it. When will they eat? When will it finish? How long does it last for? What happens if I don't like it?

c. Give comparisons

Since the brain has difficulty sifting through those mental filing cabinets, point out similarities to other events. Give the anxious brain something solid to hook on to.

d. Show them the exit

The fear of not liking something and being 'trapped' cannot be underestimated. And if you're autistic, it's easy to see why. What seems okay to everyone else might be uncomfortable to you. Uncomfortable feelings can overtake you quite quickly, you lack some capacity in calming yourself, and so you're living in fear of potential overload.

By reassuring your youngster what happens if they don't like a new event, there's more of a chance they'll try it and stick with it. But there's a limit; if the event is intrinsically autism-*unfriendly* (e.g. a lot of loud or sudden noise), then it's absolutely reasonable to request an alternative.

2. Sudden change

Autistic brains often need time to adjust to change. Because of what we mentioned earlier about new contexts being hard to assimilate, preparation and warning is needed before changes to the routine take place.

It can't be helped that from time to time pupils will have a cover teacher if theirs is off sick, but since this is bound to happen, it can be predicted and your youngster prepared for that probability.

You might not know exactly which stand-in you'll be getting, but at least you'll understand the process of what happens if a teacher is off sick. Your child's questions can then be tackled well in advance.

As we've said elsewhere in this book, letting staff know that advanced warnings of change are always welcome will remind them to avoid this kind of barrier.

3. 'Trip-wire' practices

When it comes to daily practices, schools need to take care not to set the autistic child up for a fall.

For instance, if the school needs signed paperwork and relies on a child to remember this, if they have difficulties with short-term memory, the result could be a tearful and anxious child.

Although cushioning someone a little too much can impede the development of independence, the best way to support that independence is to introduce it *gradually* with some fail-safe procedures, rather than relying on it at a critical time, such as just before a school trip!

As Gareth often says, schools shouldn't park the resilience within the child, but consider what systems and structures can do to support them. Resilience should be about the environment, systems and other people, not the young person.

So parents and carers, communicate with the school and ask that you are told about important forms, rather than have them left languishing unopened in the bottom of the school bag (oops!). We suspect parents of autistic teenagers may not be the only ones experiencing problems here. The difference is the result of that lack of communication can cause huge distress in the case of an autistic child.

Parents can also help by supporting young people to use their phone for reminders or access special apps such as the Picturepath visual scheduling app which helps with planning (see Appendix 2: References and Resources). Wipe-off charts and calendars at home, as we've already mentioned, can also be useful. Orkid Ideas creates portable visual resources for reminders. Our Boards is another useful community interest company producing visuals. And yes, ensure that important reminders are always visual, not just verbal.

4. The 'all or nothing' mindset

Most of us understand that practice makes perfect. However, if you're autistic, you may *not* quite understand this concept.

If you're autistic and you love a particular topic, your expertise in it may have come pretty easy to you! Autistic people can have incredible focus and energy with something they enjoy.

Busy localised brain activity means that once something is familiar, things just get better and better, with more information 'hooking' on to what's already there.

While this is great, some of the longer-range connections in autistic brains may not be so good at 'talking' to each other.

How does this translate in terms of learning?

It means that generalising and categorising can be quite difficult. Remember what we mentioned earlier about problems in compiling information from various 'filing cabinets' in the brain? This is why.

It is, in fact, far more complex than that, as you can probably guess. If you want to read more about this area, do pick up Peter Vermeulen's invaluable book *Autism as Context Blindness*. The author explains connections in great depth, and will probably not thank us for drawing out one key phrase from a very detailed chapter, but in simple terms we love this analogy:

> It seems that the 'orchestra' of the autistic brain has no conductor; in addition the musicians cannot co-operate well with each other. Still there are some talented players who, when they play solo, play extra ordinarily well.

> *Peter Vermeulen,* Autism As Context Blindness *(2012)*

An autistic pupil may find some things incredibly easy to learn (localised brain activity) and struggle with others (coordinated long-range connections).

The trick is to 'hook' the unfamiliar material on to the familiar, which is why using a keen interest can work so well when it comes to learning something new.

Unfortunately, many schools aren't aware of this.

You can perhaps see why the 'practice makes perfect' encouragement might be lost on our autistic mainstreamers. Their experience has taught them: 'I'm either really great at this or I struggle.'

As a parent or carer, it can be quite hard to watch this jagged profile of achievement without being tempted to iron it out a bit. And it's the same for teaching staff who don't have a great understanding of autism.

The problem is, when this person doesn't have additional learning disabilities, you could be forgiven for asking yourself why they struggle to learn.

Well, although they may not have 'learning disabilities' in a diagnostic sense, they do have learning *differences*.

As parents and education practitioners, we do need to understand that autistic brains don't operate in the same way as non-autistic ones.

The 'just try harder' argument doesn't work on some people, not because they're lazy, but because their brain finds it difficult to engage in something that doesn't have a familiar hook.

The new information simply can't find anywhere to land – it has no category for filing! So finding those familiar hooks becomes very important.

Introducing something gradually and giving an idea time to 'bed in' through repetition is also important, as is using visual methods for learning rather than simply teaching through talking.

RESPONSES CAUSED BY THE 'ALL OR NOTHING' MINDSET

- Catastrophising when a piece of work goes wrong, scribbling it out or ripping it up.
- Giving up without trying.
- Getting very angry at themselves for not instantly grasping something.

What can we do?

- ★ Chat to your child about how their brain works very fast in some areas but how, in others, learning does require practice, repetition and time.

- ★ Explain that this isn't caused by lack of intelligence but by a different way of thinking and learning. This helps to reduce anxiety about learning.

- ★ Plenty of reassurance is needed about mistakes being an essential part of learning. Point out your own mistakes as you make them!

- ★ Chat to your child's TA about 'hooking' learning on to something familiar and using visual methods of reinforcement, such as watching YouTube clips or uploading programmes they can watch repeatedly.

- ★ Using special interests to explain new concepts can help to relax your child (it can't be underestimated how powerful relaxation is for learning!) and also help them to find a place in their mind for the new information to settle.

5. Accepting feedback

How come some autistic pupils don't seem to like it when they're given feedback? If you tell yourself that you're either great or rubbish at something, and there's no grey area for learning in between, then it follows that feedback will feel like criticism.

The methods used for feedback are also sometimes likely to cause adverse reactions:

- ★ Issuing stark instructions can cause panic to set in. A youngster's poor self-regulation means that internal soothing language is not helping out when it's needed.

- ★ Lots of verbal feedback may be too much to process.

★ Autistic pupils may feel socially humiliated in the face of feedback; they don't want to be singled out.

RESPONSES CAUSED BY DIFFICULTY ACCEPTING FEEDBACK

- Not listening attentively when being given advice.
- Saying 'I know, I know, I know' when clearly they struggle!
- Being 'rude' to the person giving the feedback.

What can we do?

One of the most useful strategies Debby learnt as a parent was to use a collaborative approach when problem-solving. In this she was greatly influenced by the work of Canadian speech and language pathologist Dr Heather MacKenzie, author and creator of the SPARK programme, which stands for Self-regulation Program of Awareness and Resilience in Kids. (See Appendix 2: References and Resources for details of her books.)

Working in collaboration with a child means that you shift from a dictatorship to a democracy:

How are we going to solve this? Let's chat ideas.

There's a reason this works so well and here comes one of Debby's analogies...

Mostly, we deliver information to our children in much the same way as we load a washing machine. Open the door, shove it all in and hope for the best.

Autistic children are more like those ticket machines at gaming arcades that 'eat' strips of tickets. They have to take in information at their own speed; otherwise, a jam occurs.

Saying 'This is how you solve it...' isn't allowing processing to occur at the child's own pace.

If, however, you invite a person's thoughts and respond to them, they are able to use their own inner 'hooks' to learn new information.

This is important – it is the lack of familiarity and inability to categorise new information that can make learning difficult for autistic youngsters.

> *It is the lack of familiarity and inability to categorise new information that can make learning difficult for autistic youngsters.*

If ideas and suggestions come from them first, the new information isn't as threatening and doesn't require so much extra processing.

To illustrate how this works, we can recall a conversation we had with one parent who said she couldn't get her son to put down his gaming console for homework.

After an initial discussion about the importance of 'recharging' straight after school, Debby suggested a countdown timer to her. Countdown timers act as independent referees and can be extremely effective visual reminders.

The response was: 'He'd never accept that idea.'

That may be true; it depends on how the idea is suggested.

If you say, 'I'm going to buy you a Time Timer to help you know when it's time to do your homework', the default answer to this threatening unknown could be a nice, safe 'No, I don't want it'.

The collaborative approach involves:

a. Outlining the problem from the child's viewpoint
In this case, chatting about what a nuisance it is that mum nags about homework...and how annoying it must feel. Using this approach, the child's brain orientates towards the problem, giving them some motivation to overcome it.

b. Pondering the happy end point of a solution
The conversation moves on to how we could stop that from happening. The child's brain is now gearing up at its own pace towards considering solutions.

c. Asking the child for their thoughts

What could solve the problem? Hmm, what about a gadget that automatically tells the child how much time is left. Would it work? Nothing is imposed. All ideas are considered.

d. Considering a potential solution

In some cases, it's a nice idea to whisper the solution. 'I've found there actually is a gadget that can do this. It's called a Time Timer.' Whispering excites curiosity. Where there's curiosity and calm, kids can make space for new information. That's because curiosity comes from them, not you. Don't overuse the whispering, though; otherwise, it will cease to be effective!

e. Using their own language

It's great to use words that are in the child's own vocabulary, like 'gadget' and 'life hack', when solving problems.

f. Examining the options from a distance

Do they think some autistic people might find it easier to be told it's time to do something by a gadget rather than a parent? We view the problem-solving tool as a matter of scientific interest, something to be reviewed for other people, because it distances us from having to accept it or reject it for ourselves.

g. Allowing processing time

Much as you'd love your child to jump up and down and say ,'Yeah! Great idea!', you may need to give them time to take on board the implications of a new idea. Illustrator and author Alis Rowe said: 'I do not like to confirm things because then the thing becomes a reality. The reality tends to involve a lot of effort, and always involves a large amount of anxiety.'

This method allows time to orientate towards a new idea with less resistance. Thinking time is also a powerful tool; the sudden imposition of solutions can feel very threatening.

Before you start to say this is all very cunning manipulation of your child, it really isn't, we promise you. If you're making your way into your house from the side gate, it isn't wrong – it's just not the front door. In fact, if we had to give the approach a name, we'd call it 'The Side Gate Approach'. Maybe think of that image next time you're about to introduce a new idea!

Autistic kids sometimes act against their own interests because of the level of processing a new idea involves. It's easier to reject it.

By taking your time and theirs, you are allowing them to become receptive when you feel it may be in their own interests.

If, after that, they still say no, then you've given the idea a fighting chance – and so have they. At least you know it's a genuine 'no' rather than a knee-jerk reaction.

When issuing feedback, it's great to start with information that comes from the young person. 'Hmm, I wonder why that didn't work? What do you reckon we could try next?'

Debby's favourite method of tackling the answer 'I don't know' comes from American psychologist and TV personality Dr Phil McGraw. 'Well, if you *did* know, what would it be?'

Rather than instructing your child, think of them as a co-worker who requires tact and diplomacy.

Incidentally, Dr MacKenzie suggests sitting next to rather than behind a child when you're working together to enhance that collaborative feeling.

When critiquing our own work, it's essential that we have an idea of what 'good' looks like. As autistic people work much better from solid references rather than vague abstracts, one successful method is to show them what a successful piece of work looks like, and why.

It's also important to show what 'adequate' and 'not good enough' look like. Indeed, you can never perform at your best unless you know the parameters according to which you are working!

Write it down or use a visual so that they can make repeated visits to their reference. Showing what a good example of work looks like also means that a teacher doesn't have to focus on what's lacking, but can focus on the positives.

When receiving feedback – either from you or a teacher – our kids may not automatically realise that mistakes are an essential part of learning.

No author has ever written a book without drafting it first ('especially us', says Gareth who is constantly changing things and never 'finished'!). Even buried among the ancient ruins of Egypt are examples of practice sculptures that never made it to the pharaohs' tombs!

> *Mistakes? Even buried among the ancient ruins of Egypt are examples of practice sculptures that never made it to the pharaohs' tombs!*

As a parent, you may be tempted to dive in and help correct attempts that aren't going so well. Before you do, check that your words don't judge an attempt that hasn't been successful.

Instead, a gentler approach is:

I can see why you tried it that way...

Yes, that would have been my first thought too...

That was a great idea. Can you see why it didn't quite work out?

Reward the process of thinking, rather than purely the outcome.

6. Perception of pressure

Because of the quick anxiety response in autistic people, demands from teachers – designed to boost motivation in reluctant teens – can have a catastrophic effect on our autistic learners.

You know the sort of thing, because you've no doubt had to peel your child from the ceiling on the days when these phrases have been used:

Your deadline for this work is next Monday; don't miss it!

This exam is in five weeks – you must put the work in now.

I don't want to hear any excuses about why you couldn't complete this.

That's not motivating for an autistic child. That's quite the opposite. In fact, for any child with high anxiety it's the opposite, not just autistic pupils.

Once the 'catastrophising' button has been set to red alert, it can be hard to calm down – again, problems with self-regulation (the ability to calm those rising inner feelings) play a part. Trying to change things at a moment of crisis is absolutely the wrong time to do it.

In addition, autistic children are highly sensitive to the emotional body language of those around them, and an anxious teacher communicating anxiety to her class is often a sure-fire way of distressing them.

This is what Gareth refers to as 'emotional contagion' and it's a very real barrier for autistic pupils. Sensing high emotion in others can cause dysregulation in autistic children.

Want a calm autistic kid? Surround them with calm adults. We can't emphasise this enough.

Sure, as a parent you may not be able to choose teaching staff. It doesn't hurt, however, to explain at the start that when timetables are compiled, your child responds best to very calm, low-key adults.

RESPONSES CAUSED BY STRUGGLING WITH PERCEIVED PRESSURE

- Catastrophising, panicking, 'over-rushing' or speaking of failure.
- Asking of themselves far more than someone else asked of them.
- Explosive reactions to what looked like a simple instruction.
- Wanting to walk out.
- Shutdowns, when a pupil becomes unresponsive or uncooperative.
- Responding to a teacher raising their voice by the child raising their own voice, too, and possibly going the extra mile with this one in terms of volume...

Pressure is not something that is actually real, of course. It's based on an individual's perspective of what's being demanded of them. Sometimes children can experience far too much pressure due to having unrealistic expectations of themselves or misguided assumptions.

For example, what makes a good student? Does your child know the answer or are their assumptions way off beam?

When Bobby was asked in Year 7, 'What makes a good student?' he said:

★ understanding what was said in class

★ getting things right first time

★ getting 100% in a test

★ being interested in everything that he was taught.

No wonder he was feeling the strain!

Debby reframed his understanding by explaining that being a good student is:

★ asking the right person at the right time when you don't understand

★ being prepared to practise

★ trying your best

★ listening well even if it isn't your favourite subject.

The advice here overlaps with our hints on self-critiquing. In order to place realistic demands on themselves, autistic kids have to be given very clear expectations.

How long should they spend on a piece of homework? What is an example of good enough and not enough effort? Can those examples be written down?

Do they fully understand what's expected of them, or are they missing some vital information about why they're being asked to do something? Have they over-estimated how long a piece of work might take them? What does it involve from their perspective?

This is where having good communication with a TA can make all the difference. If you can tell them that it would be helpful to check your child's understanding of requirements before work is taken home, it can save a lot of headaches later on.

What can we do?

★ Tension at home may arise because of perceived pressures at school. If your child is unusually anxious or short-tempered, take some time to 'unwrap' the factors behind it. A 'meltdown' or explosive outburst when usually there wouldn't be one is a clue that something else has been building up.

★ Keep communicating and check regularly what your child's understanding of expectations are.

★ Tell your child not to worry about any deadlines or homework given until they can discuss it with either a teacher or yourself.

★ Be honest with your youngster that teachers use 'hurry up!' style conversations to try to galvanise the less motivated pupils in the class, but that they should just let these phrases float over them like a cloud in the sky (or other calming analogy). They may even need a pocket image to remind them of this at the crucial time!

★ Helping your child to plan their work in a visual way will break down daunting tasks into manageable ones (we'll get to that soon).

Phew – that's the first six hurdles jumped. Take a breather, and we'll get to the next six...

CHAPTER 7

JUMPING THE BARRIERS: THE NEXT SIX

You'll notice in this chapter that there's an overlap of ideas in some of these barriers. Different ways of thinking have a cascade effect, influencing a range of skills and attitudes.

Again, let's see what we can predict is likely to be a barrier, and overcome it by developing strategies and solutions alongside school.

7. Difficulty with planning

Autism affects executive functioning skills – those parts of our brain that help with planning and preparation. For this reason you can be extremely bright, but tackling a long piece of work with many constituent parts may feel out of your reach.

> ### RESPONSES CAUSED BY DIFFICULTY PLANNING
>
> - Struggling knowing where to begin, and panicking as a result.
> - A rushed or poorly executed piece of work.
> - Only part of the task being done.
> - The task not being completed in a systematic way.

What can we do?

To help with homework planning, it's a good idea to use a small wipe-off board (that's our trusty laminator again!) and create a chart with each task on it, how long it's likely to take (discuss with your youngster), the deadline and how many days left until that deadline (see Appendix 1: Useful Charts, where we've given an example as well as a blank one). Ask your child to alter the days left on a daily basis (they may need a reminder!), and to tackle the task with the least amount of time left *first*.

This decreases the pressure on parents, but, more importantly, it decreases pressure on autistic kids, too. An independent referee is far easier to work with than a person nagging at you, with all the emotional energy that needs to be digested in the process.

What you're also doing there is using your own executive functioning skills to teach your young person how to prioritise. In life, it isn't just work we need to prioritise. How many forms have you had to complete in time for a deadline? Umpteen, if you're the parent or carer of an autistic child. Life, whether we like it or not, goes much more smoothly when we are able to create priority lists for ourselves.

Incidentally, a very good digital to-do list programme is Kanban-Flow. It allows you to colour-code tasks, to create different lists for home and school, and to shift completed tasks to a 'done' pile, which is rather satisfying.

Anxiety can also be reduced by introducing visual reminders:

★ a laminated 'today' and 'tomorrow' card with immediate and future tasks reminders

★ a week-to-view diary

★ a paper calendar so that the whole month is also visible at a glance.

Digital reminders are great, but a paper visual overview of the month is helpful. Being able to see the detail of your plans but also how they fit into the wider context of the month ahead is very settling. Gareth notes that he has a physical planner on the wall and writes events and meetings on it; having an overview on an electronic system isn't the same as 'seeing' periods of time and overlaps of events.

As a carer, you can also point out to school where help with planning is needed in order to complete a task. Remind your youngster, too, that asking for help with planning doesn't mean that they can't do the work. It's like being faced with an entire chocolate cake (we wish!). Of course, you *can* try to eat it whole, but it would be tricky. You need someone with a knife to help you cut it or, better still, help you to cut it into smaller slices yourself! Knowing how and when to ask for help is important.

8. Literal thinking

Here we recall the joke:

Autism – isn't that when you take everything literally?
No, that's a kleptomaniac.

Social media is full of some amusing examples of rather literal interpretations of questions.

Can you draw this ship?
No.

How do you change centimetres to metres?
Take out centi.

Draw a plant cell.
Pupil draws a flower behind bars.

Defend your answer.
Pupil draws barbed wire and soldiers around the word 'answer'.

Or there's Debby's favourite. When a primary school maths test indicated 'Tell us how you arrived at this answer and you may get an extra mark', Bobby wrote, 'Dad told me the answer.'

The difficult landscape for literal thinkers is muddled by the fact that some non-autistic kids may well play the clown when faced with a question they can't answer and deliberately answer a question literally.

But when these funnies fly around social media, we do end up wondering how many of those answers were written by autistic kids who were just taking the question at face value.

So, at times, autistic children get mistaken for being the class clown, which upsets them (and us). They aren't being rude, they're just confused because things were not presented in a way they understood.

RESPONSES CAUSED BY LITERAL THINKING

- At times amusing interpretations of wording or phrases.
- Misunderstandings and confusion over what's required.
- Doing specifically what was asked but nothing more.
- Not understanding the context or meaning of a request.

When a literal thinker asks for clarification, the instruction to *use your common sense* is a phrase that doesn't help whatsoever.

Common sense is down to individual perception for a start. It's supposed to come from taking a new concept and applying experience from a series of previous situations and processing them together to generate a likely outcome.

None of this is easy (or even possible, in some instances).

'Common sense' becomes a lot easier for autistic people as they gain life experience (well, that is true for everyone), but asking them to use it when they are 11 or 12 may be a demand too far.

What can we do?

If you're a parent, help your child to see what's reasonable to expect of them. This could well mean that you end up explaining *why* they have been asked to do a task, so that they understand more completely what's required.

For example, if they're asked to find out some facts about Bill Gates, why isn't it enough to copy and paste his Wikipedia entry?

Again, literal thinkers will assume they've done the job to the best of their ability. If you explain the principles behind what they are being asked to do, they've got better information for knowing what's expected.

Check…check…and check understanding. And ask school to do the same!

Also, give your child ownership of their learning. Make sure that they know it's okay to ask for clarification – in fact, this is any learner's key strength.

A good strategy for teachers is to provide the instruction or task, allow 10–15 seconds' processing time, check for understanding (and maybe repeat back), then move on. Building in these routines also helps to create that 'constant consistency' mentioned previously.

> *Make sure that they know it's okay to ask for clarification – in fact, this is any learner's key strength.*

9. Inability to process group discussions

There is a modern emphasis on 'creative brainstorming' and 'collaborative thinking' in our society. If you think that this leads to better results and better creativity, we'd advise you to read Susan Cain's brilliant book on introversion, *Quiet*.

In this she points towards research that suggests that group thinking – both in the workplace and in school – isn't nearly as productive as we suppose it is. It may allow for bonding, but not necessarily for productivity.

Susan explains that those who are more introverted actually have their productivity sapped by the demands of noisy environments.

And the more she writes, the more correlations can be observed between the way autistic people work and the environments most suitable for introverts.

Not that everyone who is autistic is an introvert – they aren't. But if an autistic person has to process a lot of words and signals from other people, they may need quiet time to rebalance, which is something they have in common with introverts.

A quick reminder here of our earlier quote from Bianca Toeps:

> If you ask autistic people what they struggle with most, it's usually overstimulation they mention first.

Autistic pupils particularly struggle with 'brainstorming' exercises, partly because of social stresses and processing auditory information at speed, but also because of possible difficulties with deciphering individual voices when conversation is overlapping.

What can we do?

Make school aware that overlapping conversations can be difficult and ask for your child to be put into a smaller group, with some of the quieter pupils. As Dr Luke Beardon says, in any decision anxiety should always be taken into account.

> The mental wellbeing of the child is of paramount importance – it

should not be seen somehow as secondary to learning skills that others deem important.

Extract from Avoiding Anxiety in Autistic Children
*(2020), Dr Luke Beardon, reproduced by permission of
Sheldon Press, an imprint of John Murray Press*

10. Sensory issues

Classrooms can be chaotic, noisy places. Some pupils get a buzz out of this – it keeps them stimulated, engaged and motivated. For others, it's just too distracting and can be overwhelming. Many autistic pupils have sensitive hearing and trouble with 'filtering' out sounds that are irrelevant. Lights can be distracting or even painful. The buzz from an overhead light might be unbearably distracting.

Sensory processing disorder, whether it's experienced in a mild or a severe way, is part of autism. You can't really expect a person to overcome the difficulties and challenges they face if they are focusing on surviving the environment. As Tori Houghton and Debby explained in their children's book, *The Ice-Cream Sundae Guide to Autism*:

Brains think better when bodies are comfortable!

If you want a fabulous book on sensory matters from the viewpoint of someone who personally experiences sensory processing differences, have a read of *Making Sense* by Rachel Schneider (see Appendix 2: References and Resources).

RESPONSES TO BEING OVERWHELMED BY SENSORY INPUT

- Overstimulation leading to outbursts.
- Avoidance strategies, removing themselves from the room.
- Shutdowns, becoming quiet and unresponsive.
- Lack of focus.
- Shouting out loud at noisier pupils.

What can we do?

An occupational therapist will be able to assess sensory barriers at school and make productive suggestions about how they can be overcome. Work with school to have them visit your child at the setting. You could also speak with your GP or health visitor and they will advise you if a referral to the occupational therapy service would be beneficial.

At home, demonstrate how to ask people to stop, repeat, slow down, start again or clarify what they mean by doing exactly that every time you're confused by your youngster's description of what they found hilarious on a YouTube channel!

Make staff aware of any noise sensitivities at an early opportunity. Positioning in the classroom can be helpful if distractions get too much, as well as staff being aware that additional noises from projectors or air conditioning may be distracting.

In Gareth's timetabling plans, he took into consideration avoiding the classrooms with noisier environments for autistic learners. In the same way that the school would timetable classes for wheelchair users on the ground floor, staff would look at suitable classrooms for a range of other requirements, too.

Together with school, you can also plan the necessary steps your child can take if they feel that the environment is getting too much for them – a quiet retreat to go to and finish work, for instance.

Simply knowing that there are measures available will help to keep things calm. This stops the anxiety associated with predicting a problem, as well as encountering the hurdle itself. We'll talk about sensory issues further when we go into greater detail about adapting the school environment in Chapter 8.

11. Teaching strategies

Remember the analogy of a washing machine? If teaching focuses on loading up information like a washing machine, much of it will be rejected. There's the problem of processing speed, together with where to store that new information. There are no hooks to place it on!

Photographer Alfie Bowen (more from him later) has shared some very good insights here:

> I remember so many years of my mainstream education were spent sitting in a class with other students, being taught at their level rather than at mine, and that experience had a significant impact on me and my educational journey – I got frustrated, lost interest and withdrew not just educationally but also socially.
>
> This experience was a direct result of the educational system – schools are too worried about exam results and their reputation rather than taking a child-by-child approach, which would ensure each child was learning at the appropriate level, meaning they would learn better, would be happier in school and develop quicker in other areas too.
>
> A school should take time to learn each child's interests and passions, rather than putting them in a system that extinguishes any individuality and churns out students who are not themselves.

Interests and passions, as we've said earlier, create great learning opportunities, and if new material can be connected to something already familiar, it starts to make sense and to be categorised.

If information is mainly verbal, only so much can be taken in before it starts causing a queue in the brain, followed by a backlog and a traffic jam.

You can be academically able and still unable to process incoming auditory-only information at the same speed as your peers.

This accounts for much information being missed and all the ensuing anxiety that this causes.

In fact, moments of extreme dysregulation are often preceded by a lot of verbal demands, as we mentioned previously.

For a better understanding of processing, here's another trusty analogy.

Think of the autistic brain as a museum only open to the public by prior arrangement with the management. Inside the museum, everything is neatly ordered and categorised just the way the management likes it.

If you open the museum up with no warning and just dump a load of artefacts at the door, they won't get categorised; they'll just get thrown out.

Because of difficulties in categorising and arranging information, unfamiliar material needs time to 'bed in'. To be unpacked, looked at, considered and given its own place.

Auditory information, when given just once with a load of distractions nearby, just doesn't give the brain that much time. This is why home education can be great for autistic kids; the teacher goes at a tailor-made pace and can alter the method of delivery.

Good schools provide visual information for *all* pupils, knowing that this kind of input is less stressful – and they provide it even during sessions such as PE which are normally associated with shouted verbal instructions and lots of background noise!

What can we do?

Have regular chats with your youngster's school about how they can reinforce information in a visual way. Ask for visual resources if not enough are being provided. If you're buying any materials to support your child with learning – books, for instance – take into account the visual aspect of them, and perhaps ask your child what they think before you buy something.

12. Exam focus

The pressure of exams can cause many people to crumble, and those with high anxiety are particularly at risk. This doesn't only affect performance in the exam itself, of course, but learning in the run-up as well, as the spectre of doing badly looms large. This actually acts as a block to soaking up new information.

> Exams are widely regarded as extremely challenging experiences for autistic children, and I was no different. I re-took my GCSEs several times, and would be deflated when the results came back each time; now I realise that this didn't mean I was unintelligent, it just meant

that I was forced into a system that failed to highlight my intelligence. (Alfie Bowen)

What can we do?

When choosing subjects, ask school about the assessment and exams, find out what the 'end game' is at the start. We fervently hope that ongoing assessment will always be a substantial part of gaining qualifications in the future, as many other pupils also don't show their capabilities under exam pressure on a specific date.

At home, the first thing that you can do is take the pressure off, by stressing that what's important to you is learning, rather than results.

Support your child by helping them to break up revision into a traffic light system. Green for topics that they feel confident with, amber for those they're unsure of and red for those they haven't grasped yet. TAs can help with this.

Rather than asking your child to focus purely on 'red' topics, get them to start each revision session with a green one. The confidence and momentum built up this way can help children overcome more difficult topics. So start easy and build up a head of steam!

Think about your child's focus and energy, and spend short bursts of time focusing on difficult topics, with regular rest breaks maybe on a favourite Xbox or Switch game!

Revision timetables are important for everyone, but maybe even more so for those children who struggle when they lack routine. Adapt the homework chart for revision, and decide between you and your child how long they can comfortably spend focusing. It's better to have a focused quarter of an hour with breaks than two hours of constant distraction.

Exams can be made less stressful with adaptations. If a reduced timetable has already been agreed to start with, this can also help, of course. Having key staff in school who are knowledgeable about access arrangements and how to apply the various adjustments is key; they are worth their weight in gold! It is also important that any such adjustments for exams should be part of the 'usual way of working', and therefore should be normal routine and practice. Again, you guessed it: being proactive here is important.

> ## TIP
> ## Barriers vary!
> Barriers can vary from day to day. A youngster who has been up part of the night or under additional stress in the morning will have fewer resources to cope with the day ahead than one who is well rested and well regulated when they leave home.
>
> As a parent, it's really important to note what your child's ability to cope is likely to be like that day, and communicate it to the school.

About homework

While not exactly a learning obstacle, homework can highlight some of the key hurdles that we've spoken about in the last two chapters.

To understand the problem that autistic children have with homework, you only need to look at the word itself. It requires a child to take a task that they are used to doing at school and perform it in a completely unrelated setting. Combined with that is a deadline.

Added to this is usually an extra ingredient – your own anxiety as a parent. Will they fall behind if they don't do it? Will they get into trouble and, if so, will that cause extra battles, extra stress...?

It's really important that you tackle the subject of homework with school at an early stage, so that there's an understanding between you and you won't end up with unnecessary battles at home.

Points to discuss

★ Can school be flexible with the amount of homework expected?

★ Could time be made available in the school day for them to complete it when support is available? (Hulme Hall School in

Stockport has a homework club which helps tremendously – see Chapter 14.)

★ Agree with your child's teacher how much time should be spent on homework.

★ Make teachers aware that a definite expectation, such as completing a series of questions, is much easier for an autistic child than tasks involving imagination or open-ended research. These tasks are more vague; it's tricky to know when they are 'completed'.

★ Discuss with your child's teacher whether it's okay for your child to type work if handwriting is a problem or slows them down. The twinning of a motor skill demand with executive functioning ones can be too much for many and truly exhausting.

★ Discuss adapting homework so that, where practical, it uses your child's interests as a motivator.

This advice comes from an *AuKids* feature 'Homework: How to Win the Battle Without Making Enemies' (Issue 47); a link to the full article is included in Appendix 2: References and Resources.

If your child does struggle with homework, use a planner, and whatever you do, don't let the stress over it build up. If it's consistently an issue, this indicates that there are consistent problems associated with it, which need to be investigated.

After the hectic environment of school, autistic teenagers need more time to recharge than others. It's vital that they access this down time, and so the more homework that can be completed in school hours, the better. This is why discussing a reduced timetable at the beginning of your child's secondary school career can be truly beneficial to their wellbeing.

If the thought of a reduced timetable gives you anxiety, think of how much you've learnt since being at school. Then consider how much you now remember from your secondary school lessons. Life is a learning platform – learning doesn't begin and end with school, and an education isn't incomplete if an entire curriculum isn't covered. Autistic individuals have a tremendous capacity for taking in information, in their own space and time. This will continue as they mature.

It's not just about the number of qualifications they achieve. It's whether they have an adequate stepping stone for the next step of their journey, and whether in the process their wellbeing remains intact.

Life is a learning platform – learning doesn't begin and end with school.

CHAPTER 8

A NEW VISION: THE SATURATION MODEL

Now, although the last few chapters have been dedicated to giving you a rundown of some common hurdles and how to prevent them, prevention is *always* better than cure. This is why the first chapter of our book has given you a good idea what to look for in a mainstream setting.

We've lived with a casual, invisible form of inequality for so long, however, that many of you reading this may not be aware that there is any other way of providing mainstream schooling.

Is the best we can hope for to sign up for a mainstream school that has well-meaning staff and hope that they are reasonably flexible?

Well, the answer is no. That isn't the best you can hope for. There is far, far better.

Our problem as parents, according to Debby, is that if we don't believe something is practically or financially possible, then we are pretty unlikely to look for it, ask for it or indeed be instrumental in making it happen!

In this chapter, we'd like to share with you what a realistic, cost-effective, inclusive culture looks like. We're going to talk about a 'model' for success developed by Gareth D. Morewood and his research collaborators, Professor Neil Humphrey and Dr Wendy Symes – a model now practised in schools worldwide thanks to Gareth's extensive training... plus constantly going on about it wherever he goes.

We aren't intending to describe this to increase your frustration with your existing mainstream school, but to show you that it really is possible and that your child deserves it.

In essence, Gareth and his colleagues' Saturation Model means simply following the social model of disability. This is a way of viewing the world which says that people are disabled by barriers in society, not by their impairment or difference. In contrast, the medical model of disability, to which mainstream schools can unwittingly subscribe, says people are disabled by their impairments or differences. Under the medical model, these impairments or differences should be 'fixed' or changed by medical and other treatments, even when the impairment or difference does not cause pain or illness.

The medical model of disability is abhorrent to us as authors, as attempts to 'fix' or 'normalise' autistic people can prove extremely harmful if the reasons for their responses aren't fully understood. As we explained in Chapter 5, often when we try to 'normalise', we're taking away some really effective coping mechanisms.

The good news is that the social model of disability is gaining ground and as a society we're beginning to adapt. Now all we need is for our schools to take on board the lessons learnt elsewhere.

If you have a good relationship with your child's school, or sit on their governing body as the SEN or parent governor, you may well be able to influence the direction things take, especially if we can recommend you some good training to point them in the right direction!

With Gareth and his colleagues providing the vision, and frontline experience proving its efficacy, we hope that anyone reading this book may be able to steer more practitioners into following this model. A model, by the way, that makes things *easier*, not harder, for everyone in the community.

And don't worry – you don't have to remember this entire chapter to persuade anyone that the Saturation Model is worthy of looking at. Just look up Gareth's introduction at: www.youtube.com/watch?v=qXTBY-WH9JA.

Gareth, Neil and Wendy developed the Saturation Model in 2011 as part of an Economic and Social Research Council (ESRC) project with the University of Manchester. In essence, its aim is to create a 'level playing field' for autistic learners at mainstream school by setting up practices that make for automatic inclusion.

The model was initially developed with the sole purpose of including autistic pupils who had been excluded from or were unable to attend previous educational settings. It turned out to be so successful, however (100% of its participants went on to education, employment or training when they left school at 16), that it became the basis for the Low Arousal Supporting Educational Resilience (or LASER) approach developed through the training company Studio III in the UK.

Now an education specialist at this company, Gareth trains mainstream schools, specialist settings and individuals globally in its practices.

The Saturation Model was already well underway at Gareth's school when Debby's son Bobby joined in Year 7, and he was able to benefit personally. According to Debby, this secondary provision was a beacon of good practice, and for her it was part of the reason why Gareth's input for this book was so essential.

Those phone calls home Debby was expecting never happened. Why? Because the school was set up to know and predict Bobby's anxiety triggers, and systems were in place accordingly. The strong emphasis on being proactive and working with families was a key part of this, as we've emphasised so much until this point.

WHAT IS THE SATURATION MODEL?

The word 'saturation' is deliberately used to emphasise the need for autism-friendly principles and practices to run through every aspect of school life, just as the word 'Blackpool' runs through a stick of rock. This isn't patchy practice dependent on clued-up members of staff or one particularly good area of learning; this 'constant consistency' creates a background level of calm.

It means that the nervous system of an autistic pupil can 'stand down' from being on red alert all the time. In this less anxious state, they are far more able to cope with the occasional challenges that may arise.

The beauty of the Saturation Model is that it becomes part of school culture. But this means that a structure has to be in place for it, as well as effective planning.

The following graphic demonstrates the core principles of the Saturation Model. We'll look at each aspect in turn.

Figure 8.1 The Saturation Model (Morewood, Humphrey and Symes 2011)

THE AGENT OF CHANGE

The agent of change stands in the middle of the model, ensuring that each aspect of this system is consistently implemented.

In countless schools we've visited, if you were to draw a diagram relating to influence when it came to inclusion, the SENCo would be at the side of it, championing great outcomes where possible but not affecting very much outside of their own orbit.

The Saturation Model means that rather than the inclusion champion being a small moon circling a large planet, they become central. Oh yes! That important!

Typically, the agent of change would be the SENCo within a school, but it can also apply to the primary educator – parent, carer or teacher. They don't need to have a senior role in the school, but they have to be in a position where their ideas can be influential across the setting.

The agent of change pushes thinking and practice forward, and can often be met with resistance. They need to have the energy, humour, interpersonal skills and resourcefulness to be a 'solution broker'.

DEVELOPING THE SCHOOL ENVIRONMENT

In following the social model of disability, the Saturation Model requires that we focus on things that are within our gift to influence and change, rather than parking the perceived 'problem' with the child.

This means taking into careful consideration what we can do to minimise external stressors. Environmental factors we need to consider as part of the Saturation Model are:

★ **Emotional environment**

It's perhaps easy to forget that difficulty with self-regulation is an inherent part of autism. When a chaotic, noisy or stressful environment provokes a 'survival' response, it's difficult for an autistic youngster to self-calm. This is why it's so important for the environment around them to be calm and consistent.

You may remember us explaining Gareth's concept of

'constant consistency' in Chapter 5. Having only pockets of calm and consistency (certain lessons, before school, in the taxi home, etc.) simply gives a moment of relief from other, more chaotic times of the day. Creating a continuous, positive experience is the key to unlocking success.

In order to achieve this, it's essential for the school setting to take what Gareth calls 'corporate responsibility' for the environment, sharing the job of creating systems that complement good practice at every point in the school day.

While the phrase 'holistic approach' tends to be horribly overused (and you know how we hate jargon), it's very important when considering the emotional environment. In daily practice, Gareth often talks to students about their experience of an entire day – not school and home separately, or lessons separately from break/lunchtimes. If the youngster is in a peaceful lesson before lunch, but worried about the stampede to lunch afterwards and the noise in the canteen, they will be less well placed to perform at their best in that lesson, even if that environment itself is unproblematic.

As well as this, the personal effort required on the part of an autistic young person to address these concerns can be exhausting. This might mean fewer coping mechanisms at their disposal later in the day, or at home later, fuelling the common refrain from teachers: 'They're all right in school, no idea why they're so difficult at home.'

Consistency, as we've mentioned, means policies being married up with procedures. As we've already said, no one is harmed by calm, consistent, positive approaches. Nobody fights when they are feeling calm and relaxed, but calm environments require consistency – and calm – from every adult working at a mainstream setting.

An essential part of preparing a consistent approach is collaboration with families. This is why it's so important that you enjoy a positive working relationship when things are going well, so that there can be an open discussion on the days when the picture hasn't been as rosy.

Families may not have all the answers, and teachers may scratch their heads, too, but your pooled experience will bring more in the way of solutions than just one person's reflections. It's essential also to listen to the voices of young people themselves, finding out what is challenging for them and designing solutions together.

The topic of creating a positive emotional environment is substantial and a large part of it is down to staff interaction styles. More about that later in this chapter.

★ **Social environment**

Schools can make the social environment more inclusive by proactively engaging with young people and families to find out the student's interests. Social development can then be supported through the provision of lunchtime clubs or extra-curricular activities based on those areas of interest. Supporting a student's peers to join can create positive enjoyment and allow opportunities to grow and flourish.

The Manga Club at the school where Gareth was based was one example. Some autistic students enjoyed Manga and excelled at it, and so it provided a social platform from which they had a chance to shine.

When Debby's son Bobby couldn't find peers who would chat about Pokémon, he was encouraged to form a lunchtime group at the same school, with support. This allowed him to develop a social network with like-minded peers without having to look quite so hard for them.

★ **Communication environment**

We've already mentioned some communication obstacles in Chapter 6, such as literal interpretation of instructions. It's also necessary to be aware that concepts such as 'analysis' (often but not exclusively used in English lessons) are rather abstract in nature. It always pays, and never patronises, to check understanding and ensure that instructions are unambiguous.

Students may need some extra help in understanding exactly what's meant by terms such as 'discuss' or 'show evidence' (here is where pre-learning terminology as part of additional support can come in handy). Creating frameworks that they can use repeatedly can also be really helpful, rather than presenting autistic kids with a single broad instruction.

Great communication from teachers is especially important when youngsters are bringing work home. We've heard from perplexed parents trying to find clarity in a piece of homework that they can barely interpret themselves, and all the while their youngster is becoming more and more anxious that their homework won't be 'right'.

The solution is simple. Before the autistic student leaves the classroom, teachers can check in with them quickly: 'Can you repeat back to me what you think you'll need to do for this homework? Let's check you're okay with it.'

In Chapter 6 we also mentioned that when giving instructions, teachers need to be mindful of the difficulty that autistic students can experience in processing and storing a lot of auditory information. The presence of back-up visual communication (videos, presentations or website info) that can be revisited repeatedly at a learner's own pace will more often than not be beneficial to everyone, not just autistic learners.

Allowing processing time when asking questions or having a conversation is also a small but vital adjustment to the learning setting, especially as processing time may be longer when a youngster is stressed.

★ **Physical (sensory) environment**

One of the biggest challenges facing schools is adapting the physical environment in order to reduce sensory stressors, which can, of course, vary from pupil to pupil. As we said earlier, brains think better when bodies are comfortable! When classrooms are large and full of teenagers, this is no small challenge.

In creating timetables for autistic students, Gareth would take into account the environment and plan for it; if a classroom had a noisy air conditioner and a student was sensitive to it, it was avoided in their timetable. The idea of 'constant consistency' means that all aspects of a child's learning are taken into account at the planning stage.

Teachers reading this may think that physically adapting the environment may be too hard, but it's often the really small changes that count for a lot, such as positioning a child in a quieter area of the classroom free from distractions.

Sarah Calvert, SENCo and inclusion coordinator at Oakwood Integrated Primary School in Belfast, developed a sensory audit and wrote about it in a blog for Optimus Education – you'll find a link to the blog in Appendix 2: References and Resources for this chapter. The blog also includes a link to her child-friendly sensory audit. It points out both the obvious and more subtle aspects of the environment and makes useful suggestions on how to adapt and improve it.

PEER EDUCATION AND AWARENESS

In Chapters 9 and 10 we'll be writing about friendships and peer relationships. Schools that follow this model provide students with accurate information about autism and other neurodevelopmental conditions.

Good peer education should be used to increase understanding of autism and provide guidance on how students can interact with and support their fellow students.

Schools should also celebrate the achievements of autistic individuals and use lived experience for their information, while ensuring that all aspects of the curriculum reflect a modern neurodivergent population.

Vulnerable students can be protected by their own peers, too. An example is the Circles of Friends approach, in which a small group forms a support network around a vulnerable pupil. Of course, these kinds of systems shouldn't be forced on autistic learners (and should come with a warning about *how* they can be used as part of a wider approach) but used when wanted and needed, with ideas adapted and developed for the individual as part of a personalised approach.

Ensuring this personalised approach that respects the needs and wishes of each child, rather than adopting a 'blanket policy' is a key part of the Saturation Model.

The Saturation Model promotes bullying prevention throughout the school. We'll talk about this – and how parents can influence it – in the next few chapters.

DIRECT SUPPORT AND INTERVENTION

Direct support is about assessing each child's needs and planning interventions accordingly. As well as considering their academic needs, a school should assess the need for other kinds of intervention, tailored specifically for each pupil to help them with their learning, social and personal development. What kind of interventions? Speech and language therapy to help with the development of understanding, occupational therapy in some cases to help with coordination or handwriting difficulties, educational psychology and sometimes other psychological intervention work.

It's important to note yet again that the Saturation Model never talks about a broad-brush approach. Not every autistic child will need the same kinds of intervention, and interventions should most definitely *not* be about normalising or fixing an individual but be part of a personalised package.

As well as staff training for interventions (say, to help a child with their self-calming), Gareth's school also used a team of in-house specialists.

These members of staff made expert interventions easy and a regular part of the school curriculum, and were able to subtly support key areas while on break duty or having lunch with pupils.

University students training in these areas were sometimes employed in addition to existing staff to give the school less costly but very beneficial input and to prepare helpful strategies and work with families.

FLEXIBLE PROVISION

Despite sharing common characteristics, no two students are the same. Being flexible around timetables, the use of equipment, quiet areas and unstructured times is essential for autistic pupils to be able to make the most from their schooling.

In some cases, flexibility of provision may even extend to students having dual-roll placements, sharing time between two settings, through the development of formal partnerships between mainstream and specialist schools. Gareth first established these formal partnership arrangements in the early 2000s; although many settings continue to say this isn't possible, from our first-hand experience, it most certainly is!

Children and young people's daily timetables need to be adaptable and allow time for them to withdraw from lessons in which they feel that the cognitive and/or social demands are too high. Scheduling these moments of escape and calmness (yes, proactively!) provides an excellent opportunity for the sorts of specialist intervention we have just mentioned.

For instance, Bobby had a reduced timetable. He replaced French with group speech and language therapy sessions. In terms of his own growth and learning, the Saturation Model allowed the school to look beyond purely academic attainment and to his wider development.

Bobby's PE theory lessons were replaced by 'free periods' to enable him to catch up with homework during school time with support, as well as pre-learn new vocabulary or concepts as required. He also used free sessions for winding down with a meditation app. Bobby still joined in PE practical sessions, with the option of using the gym as an alternative. During PE, Bobby's teachers also gave him alternative options right from the start of the lesson – and even larger bats to help him improve his coordination!

When the class had to write about women's rights in history, Bobby's teacher was aware (due to his single-page student passport, distributed to each teacher) that Bobby found lengthy writing assignments physically very taxing, and so he interviewed him on the subject instead, and marked him accordingly.

This constant prediction of potential stressors meant that Bobby was less often in the sort of state that would require him to spot his heightening emotions and engage self-regulation strategies, all of which is very draining.

POLICY DEVELOPMENT AND EMBEDDING PRACTICE

In order to allow for flexible provision, it's really important that policies allow for differentiated practice. For instance, a uniform policy that dictates blazers should be worn at all times should be worded in such a way that allows for relaxation in the case of students with particular sensory needs.

To use another example, rather than assuming no autistic pupil will ever be late as a result of disruption or distress before leaving for school, the school should have measures in place for what to do if this happens (no knee-jerk responses). Allowing pupils time to get settled in a designated area before re-joining their classes creates far more calm. Punishments for lateness can create significant additional stress; the point of the Saturation Model is that this doesn't have to be the case. Policies have allowed for it, and peer education has ensured that others don't deem it as unfair. Policy should not react to situations, but rather practice should be supported by carefully considered policy.

The 'agent of change' has an important job to do in ensuring that policies do allow for reasonable adjustments and are co-designed in a supportive and positive manner.

Since the flexible late system was automatically in place for Bobby, Debby knew that it wasn't the end of the world if he needed to calm down before school for any reason. There wouldn't be endless explanations and apologies. Bobby knew exactly where to go when he got in, ready for the second period. This made Debby somewhat less anxious when delayed by an outburst and in turn – since emotion is contagious – it calmed Bobby, too. Great communication meant that she could quickly warn school what was happening, too.

TRAINING AND DEVELOPMENT OF STAFF

If teachers don't understand autism, then despite their willingness to do the best for their autistic pupils, their efforts may be undermined by a lack of engagement from the pupils themselves.

For this reason, training in autism is essential, preferably from an autistic person themselves. Often ex-students and older peers were hugely powerful in supporting this, particularly with less formal sessions and ongoing discussions or as part of continuing professional development.

The Saturation Model advises that training should be regular and ongoing. As well as helping create good practice, training also increases teachers' sense of personal responsibility for the learning of all students, particularly autistic learners. Regular twilight training sessions where staff *and* students/families shared good practice allowed for ongoing development of strategies and the development of more inclusive teaching. This was led by the Learning and Teaching team to ensure a whole-school approach, rather than being presented as a 'bolt-on' from the SEND team.

CREATING A POSITIVE ETHOS

Of course, on one level a positive ethos is down to all those aspects of a school's communication with its community that we mentioned in Chapter 1. Every time you step foot inside a new setting, you can immediately identify its culture through the messages that are displayed and the people chosen to represent it. Positive and inclusive communication plus good awareness of differences all play their part.

As with all the elements of the Saturation Model, though, schools need to consider how they can create and sustain a positive ethos. This isn't about 'toxic positivity' or tokenistic awards/rewards, but about the language we use, embedding collaboration and being solution-focused in approaches.

Simply talking about stressors and actively doing something to reduce them creates a different and more positive ethos than trying to normalise or make individuals conform.

Ensuring there is a consistent drive for positive solutions to challenges will offer valuable learning opportunities that keep the whole school approach developing, evolving and, most importantly, improving the outcomes for young people.

We don't profess to have all the answers or a magic wand for school improvement, but we do think the adaptation and application of the Saturation Model can make a difference, even if only to stimulate some thinking and debate. For if we do nothing, we end up even further behind.

THE SATURATION MODEL'S IMPACT

Since the Saturation Model creates a culture in which triggers are predicted and systems put in place accordingly, a crisis is far less likely to happen.

★ Is the canteen too noisy? If we know about it, we can choose a quieter area or a quieter time.

★ Is the bell too loud? Don't have a bell. We all have watches.

★ Is the classroom too noisy? With the help of the child's personal profile, we can predict this and create a seating plan away from noisier pupils and nearer the teacher.

★ Is writing things down creating anxiety? If we know about it, we can supply an alternative.

This is why, as a parent or carer, it's so important that you advise a school of your child's needs right at the start, enabling a proactive approach. In effect, you're helping to design your own setting informed by the Saturation Model.

REFLECTING AND HELPING CHILDREN TO REFLECT

The key to good teaching practice is self-reflection. The LASER programme of training used by Studio III incorporates not only learning about the Saturation Model but also a technique known as the low-arousal approach. This is a calm and non-confrontational approach that will allow staff to assist children who struggle with self-regulation.

As part of the approach, Gareth shows professionals in settings how to reflect on their own reactions and responses to stressful situations, acknowledging their own impact on every interaction.

For teachers, keeping things calm when a pupil is experiencing a 'fight or flight' response to the environment will help to bring that youngster into a state where they can think more productively. It may take a little patience and time, but those things are within your gift, as Gareth will testify. As SENCo, he has often sat in corridors with angry or upset teens, calmly keeping them company (from a non-confrontational distance) until they've had space and time to calm.

Self-reflection is also an important part of collaboration, both with families and with students themselves.

This can mean a teacher sitting down with an autistic youngster after a distressing day and asking them: 'What could I have done differently that would have made you feel calmer in that situation? How can I help you at those times?'

No one learns from a situation when they're highly stressed. Learning can only occur after the situation has passed and calm is renewed.

We haven't the space to go into too much detail on the low-arousal approach, but you can find details of Professor Andrew McDonnell's book at the end of this chapter and in Appendix 2: References and Resources.

THE CARER'S ROLE

You can see that a lot of the strategies in the Saturation Model require predicting possible stumbling blocks and thinking of ways to overcome them.

If, as parents and carers, we are able to do that on behalf of a school and use the knowledge we have of our children to inform their practice, we're already winning here.

Once you've set up great collaboration, using the strategies discussed earlier in this book, you have a platform from which you can discuss flexible timetabling, peer group training and avoidance of stressors.

Your own wisdom will no doubt help to educate your child's school in how successful collaboration can make for far better outcomes.

You also have a part to play in reflective approaches. The chances are that it's in the home environment, several hours after a stressful situation has occurred, when your child will be ready to reflect on what happened.

It may well be *you* having that conversation after an outburst at school (and we know it is, a lot of the time!). If you're able to do this sensitively, you'll then be ready to share some positive suggestions with school and have a productive conversation with them in the days that follow.

We have a couple of great examples to share with you here about how both teachers and parents can work together on a reflective approach.

During one lesson at secondary school, Bobby's friend was told off. Remember that emotion is contagious and, being autistic, Bobby soaked up the atmosphere like a sponge, was quickly overwhelmed by the increased level of emotion and had an outburst. He then went to the dedicated Curriculum Support room to calm down.

Once he was calmer, the teacher went to visit him. He squatted by him and said: 'I've not seen you do that before. I'll level with you, I wasn't quite sure what to do.'

As Bobby wasn't being threatened, he was able to have a calm conversation about what had happened and reflect on it. This teacher, who wasn't a member of Curriculum Support team, was using a low-arousal approach with Bobby. To be honest, the situation would have been prevented if he'd also used a low-arousal approach on Bobby's friend too, but this isn't a perfect world and we have to accept that teachers are human!

However, this just goes to show how important the Saturation Model is. We don't just keep low-arousal training to a cluster of TAs; it pervades school culture and embodies the ethos.

Following some reflection on another stressful situation, Debby worked together on a Comic Strip Conversation with her son.

Comic Strip Conversations can be very useful in gathering the correct information in the evening to share with teaching staff at a later point. As with everything, Comic Strip Conversations can be woefully misused; it is important to know how to use them and when, and the brilliant Lynn McCann at ReachOut ASC is definitely our 'go-to' here. We've included some useful information from that organisation in Appendix 2: References and Resources for this chapter.

In this approach you simply guide the child as you, or they, draw stickmen to look back on a situation and reflect on it from all angles. This way, you can physically 'see' the run-up to a situation and what thoughts accompanied it. After it, you can have a chat about what could have been done to improve the situation.

You don't have to be brilliant at artwork!

We're going to give you an example of a scribbled Comic Strip Conversation Debby had with Bobby on a day when things didn't go well. While you are both focusing on the paper and the story, the glare of attention is off the child themselves, and – much in the same way as having a stroll together – they can reflect more easily.

According to the stickman, the day started well, with Bobby happy. But then there was a lot of noise, which made him distressed (Debby showed this by stickman blocking ears). He ended up getting very dysregulated and loud, and at the same time deeply conscious of the reaction from other pupils and from an angry teacher (under Bobby's supervision, stickmen were pointing and saying, 'What's up with him?'). The teacher stickman, meanwhile, was saying, 'This is unacceptable!' We were able to reflect enough to guess that the teacher's response in this case did *not* take the calm, low-arousal form and was caused by not knowing how to handle Bobby's outburst.

Bobby later pictured himself lying on the ground, full of remorse for his actions, and also unable to focus in Geography because, as he explained, he still hadn't had a chance to apologise to the teacher concerned. We drew a thinking bubble from his head saying, 'Sorry, sorry, sorry.'

Because of this conversation, we were able to relay to school that Bobby needed to be able to have a conversation with a teacher if he had experienced a 'meltdown'; he needed 'closure'. Of course, the teacher needed a better understanding of why it had occurred, and Debby was able to approach SENCo Gareth about explaining sensitivity to noise and self-regulation.

Now the process could be used more proactively and less reactively, not to surprise you with that again!

Text conversations or instant messaging between a parent and child can also be quite helpful. Sounds bizarre, doesn't it? You're in the same house! But kids can often digest written words better than auditory ones, pause for reflection and be more open about their feelings without face-to-face contact.

Unwrapping situations in these ways and being able to see the lead-up to them was extremely helpful to Bobby, as was analysing what could be done next time.

After the Comic Strip Conversation, we wrote this Social Story™ for Bobby. When everyone's working together this well, you've got prevention *and* cure *and* reflection all going on at the same time!

If you'd like to know how to write a Social Story™, there are plenty of great books by Carol Gray who is responsible for the idea. There is also a full guide to writing one in *AuKids* Issue 15. See Appendix 2: References and Resources.

SOCIAL STORY™: WHEN OTHER PEOPLE ARE TOLD OFF

Sometimes when I am at school, children around me may get told off. My friend Andy may get told off, too.

They might get told off because they are being naughty or doing something dangerous.

Teachers sometimes shout because it stops children being naughty straight away.

My ears are a bit sensitive and I don't like people shouting. Sometimes it feels as if they are shouting at me. I don't like it.

Also I don't like people shouting at Andy because he is my friend and it upsets me.

If I start to feel upset, I can tell Miss Bentine.

If I feel that Andy has not been fairly treated and my feelings are getting too much, I should also tell Miss Bentine and show her an orange traffic light sign.

Then we can go to N2 (quiet room) and talk about what has happened.

Andy might be my best friend but he is a different person to me. If I am upset because he has been told off, I will try my best not to argue with the teacher about it.

This is because a disagreement is between Andy and the teacher. If I feel the teacher hasn't got enough information about what happened, I can tell Miss Bentine (TA).

If someone else gets told off, I will try to do some deep

breathing and tell Miss Bentine if I think my feelings are getting too big for my body.

I can still be a good friend. I can still support my friend when they are worried or upset.

People can get a bit nervous about writing Social Stories™, but remember this is your situation and your child; the best ones are tailor-made for them, and proactive, so don't be nervous. The key rule is keeping it to first-person language and to use mostly descriptive statements rather than prescriptive (bossy!) ones. This means the language isn't threatening and requires the least amount of processing. Debby used pictures for hers, although they aren't shown here. *Stories that Explain* by Lynn McCann is also a useful guide – see Appendix 2: References and Resources for full details.

Bobby rarely experienced large outbursts after this, as he was able to intervene sooner with his own strategies.

As well as children reflecting with their carers, there are also many reflective exercises that teachers, carers and other professionals can engage in to help them take stock of how a situation unfolded, and how their own behaviour may have contributed.

The Reflective Journey by Professor Andy McDonnell is a comprehensive guide for practitioners that centres around reflective practice as a key concept of the low-arousal framework. Understanding stress also means accepting that highly distressed individuals are often not in control of their behaviour.

TIP

Anyone wanting to find out more about the Saturation Model and low-arousal approaches can go to www.studio3.org and join one of their regular training events.

CHAPTER 9

TACKLING BULLYING TOGETHER

ALFIE'S STORY

Alfie Bowen took up photography when he was 16, which helped to insulate him from the constant bullying he was subjected to in his secondary education because he was autistic. His misery in secondary school resulted in several suicide attempts during his teens. Wildlife photography became his saviour.

Now a renowned photographer in his early 20s, Alfie's prints are sold in Castle Fine Art galleries all over the UK and his first hardback book of photographs was published in 2021. He's also become a high-profile wildlife ambassador on the international stage, with fans including Chris Packham and David Attenborough.

It all seems a world away from the isolation he suffered less than ten years ago, but Alfie kindly agreed to share his schooling experiences with us as we start to examine what needs to be done in order to make secondary school a more secure place for autistic teenagers.

Education was always a tough experience for me, with many people judging me because of my lack of social skills or inability to 'fit in'.

Primary school was possibly the easiest period in education because I hadn't yet realised that I was different from the majority of my peers. I went about my daily business and didn't really care about not talking to people; I was used to being in my own bubble with a wildlife magazine.

High school was like a kick in the teeth for me as it became abundantly clear that I didn't entirely fit in with the people that I was surrounded by. Getting laughed at for constantly reading about animals was a painful wake-up call, and knowing that I was no longer accepted for exploring my passion was scary.

The high school I attended had a population of over 1000 students, and I was placed in a form group of over 30 students – a scary prospect for a child who struggled to speak to one person, let alone 30.

I dreaded class time each and every day. I would spend the entire duration sitting at my desk, watching the clock hung on the wall in front of me, and praying that it would soon strike three o'clock so that I could escape and return home to my wildlife magazines.

I will always remember that class; it felt as though everyone around me was speaking a foreign language that I could not understand, and so I did not fit in at all. As I said, there were where 30 students in that class. Every lesson was with them, every minute of every day was with them…and not even one ever bothered to say 'hello'.

It was during this time that I watched and tried to listen to what the majority of those around me were discussing – cars, motorbikes, celebrities, dating – and then there was little me, only interested in wildlife. But I'd had enough of feeling alone and clock-watching, so I tried to develop an artificial interest in the more 'normal' topics of discussion amongst teenagers.

I came home from school stressed, and forced myself to research these topics, that were really of no interest to me, just so that I could attempt to chat with the others...although this ultimately failed, and I was still shunned from their discussions.

This alienation led to severe mental health issues, resulting in several suicide attempts and a refusal to leave my bedroom for over a week. I left that school a broken person. I'd given up on everything and had become very short-tempered and foul-mouthed – characteristics I hated, but struggled to control because deep down I knew for the first time that I didn't and wouldn't ever fit in.

My social skills were non-existent, and I couldn't stay in a busy room without feeling dizzy. After four court appeals, my mum got me into Centre Academy East Anglia, a small private special educational needs school in the East Anglian countryside. I went on to pass several GCSEs, six American Diploma subjects at Grade A–A* (coursework-based qualifications equivalent to A-Levels) and was appointed as the school's first head student.

Alfie's experiences are all too common. Even in schools that seem to have inclusive teaching practice, many autistic pupils feel isolated, and too many are bullied.

The switch from primary to secondary school often represents a jolt socially. In primary school, younger children who have grown up alongside autistic youngsters aren't yet aware of social differences. By the time they notice them, they've got to know an autistic child as a friend. For this reason, primary school peers are often more accepting. They experience fewer barriers caused by a label.

In secondary schools, it's a different story. How can we make these environments safe for autistic teens as well as being a place in which excellent peer relationships can flourish?

If a pupil doesn't feel safe, they can't learn, so whatever we write about, tackling this within our schools is the number-one priority.

According to 2017 research by Campbell and colleagues in Australia, significantly more autistic students reported they had been the victim of physical, verbal and social bullying (58.7% as opposed to 37.5% in non-autistic students).

This is borne out by earlier UK research in 2006 by Batten and colleagues for the National Autistic Society as part of its *Make School Make Sense* campaign. For this research, the team analysed 1400 responses from families, as well as the responses of 28 autistic children who were interviewed about their experiences. It found that over 40% of children on the autistic spectrum had been bullied at school. For children with Asperger syndrome, which was then identified separately from autism, the figure was higher, with three in five parents saying that their children had been bullied at school.

How can schools, parents and pupils themselves reduce this dismal statistic?

No school can stop bullying entirely (and we would be wary of any setting that claimed that this was the case!). What we can do, however, is to put strategies in place to significantly reduce the risk of it happening.

Although bullying is a very complex subject, with many factors influencing outcomes, four key areas in schools should be addressed in order to tackle it, according to the conclusions from research by Humphrey and Hebron, 'Bullying of children and adolescents with autism spectrum conditions: A state of the field review' (2015).

These areas are:

1. autistic students

2. their peers

3. teachers and support staff

4. school culture and climate.

1. AUTISTIC STUDENTS

Humphrey and Hebron's research indicates that helping to develop understanding around the subject of bullying can play a part in protecting autistic pupils from it. Many autistic children seem to understand what bullying is, but less so when it's happening to them. Increasing understanding can help to ensure that there isn't under- or over-reporting of bullying.

Here are some tips on how you can develop that understanding.

a. Explain bullying

In their 'state of the field' review, Humphrey and Hebron quoted an interesting study from Beaumont and Sofronoff (2008) that examined the effects of an intervention in Australia for autistic adolescents. The intervention was called the Junior Detective Training Programme. It was a seven-week course that included a computer game designed to teach emotion recognition, regulation and social interaction, as well as facilitate small group therapy sessions.

Reporting on the programme's results, Humphrey and Hebron said:

> Session content was directly relevant to bullying prevention, and included activities to help students differentiate friendly joking from bullying, and how to deal with bullying. Amongst the positive effects identified by the authors was a significant improvement in emotion management strategies in relation to bullying and teasing.
>
> *Humphrey and Hebron (2015) 'Bullying of children and adolescents with autism spectrum conditions: A state of the field review', p.854*

It seems that it would be very helpful to introduce this sort of programme into mainstream schools as part of a raft of strategies to combat bullying.

However, in the meantime, parents can do something similar for their own youngsters.

Take some time with your child to explore the difference between teasing and bullying. It's important not to assume that your child's definition of the word 'bullying' is the same as yours. In fact, don't assume *anything* where an autistic child is concerned – always check!

So, how would they recognise whether someone is being cruel and relentless or just a jokey teenager mucking about a bit?

This is difficult for autistic youngsters, and the point really is that peers should have enough understanding to be sensitive (see the section about their peers below).

Here are some questions to help your teen understand bullying.

★ **What's this person's relationship to you?**

If this is someone you don't know at all, teasing you on your appearance, body language or behaviour, or calling you cruel names, is always unacceptable.

★ **Do they stop if you ask them to?**

Good friends who are kidding around will stop if something is causing upset, rather than continuing saying the same thing when it obviously isn't appreciated. Bullies continue despite the other person showing distress. Or they seek out 'targets' especially for these kinds of negative interactions.

★ **Do they humiliate you in front of others?**

Is what they say cruel, and do they do this in social situations? Talk about how you'd define 'cruel'.

★ **Watch their body language**

Are they looking at you and laughing with you as they are say-ing something, or are they looking at others in the group and nudging them? If they are looking at others, elbowing them or giving sideward glances and smirking, they're enjoying the reaction from their friends and that's bullying. Debby demon-strated what this looked like to her son.

For more resources on bullying, see Appendix 2: References and Resources.

b. Analysing situations

If your son or daughter has been confused by a social situation, it's sometimes helpful to draw a Comic Strip Conversation that evening recreating it, before asking them what they assume other's thoughts to be (we talked about Comic Strip Conversations in Chapter 8).

This is a little work but builds great knowledge. Slowing down a social situation like this allows your child to be able to spot non-verbal clues in the environment, and to think about their own reactions and what they could have done to help themselves.

It also helps you as a parent to assess whether what your child is describing is a harmless event or harassment, and whether to take it further with school.

c. Home learning

Some families avoid both sarcasm and mickey-taking around their autistic children because parents feel they 'wouldn't get it'. If they don't get it, it's generally because they don't understand the playful nature of it, and this highlights a social skills gap that you can help them to fill.

As we're very fond of saying, home is a great practice ground for social skills. We don't mean that we expect you to sit down and have a lesson about them! Rather, knit those explanations into your daily conversations. If you're sarcastic about something, point it out and explain it, drawing attention to the tone of voice being used.

> *If you're sarcastic about something, point it out and explain it, drawing attention to the tone of voice being used.*

If you're teasing someone else in the family, point out that it's a joke. The more they hear what it sounds like and witness the accompanying body language, the more they'll be able to recognise it and, yes, eventually even use it themselves.

This *is* possible. Just because someone doesn't automatically pick up on sarcasm, this doesn't mean they can't learn what it is. Particularly in secondary school when peers can be very sarcastic and literal thinking can make you vulnerable, learning sarcasm can be an enormous help.

By the way, we wouldn't suggest teasing or using sarcasm in the family any more than you usually would do, and certainly not singling out the autistic member of the family in the name of practice! But it's helpful if rather than avoiding it when it's used, you point out the more subtle forms of humour that a literal thinker may struggle to understand.

This is subtle; it isn't 'training' autistic children. However, by providing exposure to social situations in the family home – and explanations about them – you're able to put context to situations your child may encounter in the future, or allow a reference point so that they can ask further questions as situations arise.

Bobby knows how to recognise and use sarcasm; he learnt this from his parents. He is now 18 and Debby asked him to share how he feels about mickey-taking now that he's had ample time to observe and practise it:

> You've just got to appreciate that not everything in life is to be taken seriously and you've got to have fun with yourselves and others sometimes. Take it easy, you know! These days I laugh it off if someone takes the mickey and I find it easier.

As with most social skills, what doesn't come naturally can be learnt to great effect. You're not changing who they are; you're shoring up their ability to cope with non-autistic social situations.

Learning to laugh at yourself is hard, and you need to feel confident in yourself in order to do it. Point out to your teen when they are great at something because their brain works differently; highlight the advantages of their different ways of thinking. Keep showing them examples of successful autistic adults. Always balance out your discussions about autism. Some things will be a struggle because of autism – others might be easier.

Theirs is a brain that works using a different operating system. If you'd like more guidance on chatting to your child about autism, have a look at Chapter 2 'Autism Can Change: Looking beyond the traditional definition' in Debby Elley's 2018 book *Fifteen Things They Forgot to Tell You About Autism*.

2. THEIR PEERS

Improved peer understanding was a core component of the joint paper we have talked about previously, written by the co-author of this book, Gareth, and his colleagues Neil Humphrey and Wendy Symes – 'Mainstream autism: Making it work' (2011).

The effects of peer education were also analysed in the research paper about bullying by Humphrey and Hebron, mentioned earlier in this chapter – 'Bullying of children and adolescents with autism spectrum conditions: A state of the field review' (2015).

In this piece of research, when discussing the effects of peer education in autism, the authors quoted a fascinating American study by Campbell and colleagues (2004). Campbell's research team took a sample group of third to fifth graders (ages 8-11). All of them were shown short clips of a 12-year-old male actor displaying stereotypic hand movements, body rocking, echolalia and gaze aversion. Half of them received both descriptive and explanatory information designed to educate and develop understanding of autism. The other half received no explanations ;they simply watched the videoclips.

The research found that those youngsters who were given extra explanations had improved behaviour intentions (i.e. they were more likely to say they would play with the child) in all grades and improved attitudes in both third and fourth graders.

Even without this kind of research to give us evidence, most of us instinctively know that increased education reduces fear of the unknown, no matter which minority group we're discussing.

No one emphasises the need for peer education more than those who have been on the receiving end of bullying. According to Alfie Bowen:

I have been quite vocal about my desire to see acceptance and aware-ness of people's differences taught in schools – most of the bullying I faced was caused by a lack of understanding, and education is the most powerful tool we have, and thus we must use it.

Let's talk about autism, let's promote everything that is wonderful about it, let's teach our pupils how to support their peers when they are struggling, let's promote the importance and acceptance of neu-rological diversity just as we teach the acceptance of racial diversity.

This education will not only help them as pupils in school, but also as adults in society.

Change will never come from sitting down, it comes from standing up and talking, and that is what we must do.

At Gareth's school, peer education was made a priority.

Through whole-school assemblies, peer talks in class and life edu-cation lessons developed with the special school they partnered with, his school gave a detailed explanation of what autism is, why pupils present and engage differently within the school environment, and the support that they need in order to 'create a level playing field'.

In the same school, a film of the famous autistic artist Stephen Wiltshire was played, showing him drawing St Paul's Cathedral from memory. Pupils were then asked to attempt the same in five minutes! Although there's a danger in over-promoting the notion of 'autism superheroes' (not everyone has an amazing talent, after all), this sort of exercise can fit in well as part of a package of awareness and understanding.

This secondary school also teamed up with the local specialist autism school, and a senior member of the outreach team there gave specialist, highly interactive peer training which subsequently became part of the curriculum for everyone.

We think here the word 'interactive' is important. There's nothing like experiencing a difficulty yourself in order to know how someone else feels.

So, if your school hasn't got peer training, do suggest it. The best peer training is presented by autistic people themselves!

3. TEACHERS AND SUPPORT STAFF

As we've stressed in other chapters, decent autism training ensures that staff understand the barriers we've mentioned in Chapters 6 and 7. It also ensures that they have a positive attitude and aren't inadvertently legitimising bullying by the way that they personally interact with autistic pupils (e.g. showing exasperation or impatience or ridiculing literal responses – even though we would hope that no one in their right mind would do this, it does happen!).

All staff should show understanding and acceptance, be flexible and adaptive, and encourage differences – and pupils pick up on their lead.

Humphrey and Hebron supported this in their review when quoting some 2003 research by Robertson, Chamberlain and Kasari, 'General education teachers' relationships with included students with autism'. The study found that the quality of teacher–student interactions had a bearing on peer acceptance of autistic children.

This does emphasise why it's so important when choosing a school to ask questions about the nature of the autism training undergone by their staff.

Depending upon the setting and previous emphasis, all training and development needs should be tailored to a specific context. We would suggest being very wary of 'one-size-fits-all' training and prefer an emphasis on ongoing coaching and support as part of a culture, rather than a 'one off' event.

4. SCHOOL CULTURE AND CLIMATE

As our co-author Gareth's school followed the Saturation Model, which we talked about in Chapter 8, the culture was inclusive. So, what happened in that inclusive environment to prevent bullying? Here's Gareth's advice for what smart schools can do.

a. Draw the line

Smart schools constantly promote proactive responses to bullying and give regular reminders of what unacceptable behaviour towards others is, so that children can identify and know how to report bullying.

b. Have anonymous methods of reporting

A bullying box, for instance, can encourage secret reporting of incidents, although it shouldn't be used as sole evidence. Online reporting functions, knowledge of the pastoral system and having key adults to turn to all serve to help.

c. Prevent isolation

Isolation can be reduced by making sure that unstructured time such as break and lunchtime are catered for, allowing vulnerable pupils to use the computer or library.

Schools can also provide lunchtime clubs, buddying schemes or friendship benches where children can sit if they need someone to play with. Some schools have a Circle of Friends, a small volunteer group of pupils identified to help autistic pupils with social skills and look out for them.

As a carer, you can always be proactive by asking your school to support your child in running a club on their own special interest. Many school clubs centre around team sporting games; these aren't always ideal for autistic youngsters. They rely on understanding shouted instructions in noisy environments and autism can be linked to coordination issues which make team games less attractive.

By starting up clubs for their own interests, autistic pupils can be supported to take leadership positions, build their confidence and make new friendships.

There are many things possible and adaptable, depending on the setting; it is the desire to think positively and in a solution-focused way that is essential.

d. Create a culture of inclusion

This means that difference and diversity are celebrated at every opportunity. All pupils' work is displayed and autistic children are given a chance to shine. As we stated earlier, one school had a Manga Club, in which autistic pupils took lead roles in supporting peers to develop work on projects and pieces of art. It also had a Lego™ Club run by one of its in-house speech and language therapists, which was very popular.

A culture of inclusion also means that inclusive policies are put in place that serve to benefit everyone, without singling out children because of their SEN. An example of this kind of strategy would be using paper that hasn't got a reflective shine, which would be distracting for someone with visual perception differences.

Rather than going to all the bother of sourcing two kinds of paper and singling someone out, you're simply making the playing field level with your choice of material.

e. Encourage communication

Restorative approaches, where pupils are encouraged to talk situations through with each other with support and structure, are more effective than punishment and address the root causes of bullying. Careful implementation of these approaches is vital; too often simply 'applying' them to a situation means those on the receiving end must face the other party in an inappropriate situation. It's always best to seek advice and support when implementing such strategies.

f. Tackle problems quickly

You can't always predict a situation, but once it happens, a good school will adapt quickly to prevent a recurrence. In doing so – and reflecting on what happened – they then put in place new and amended systems so that a repeat is avoided. Here is where good communication between parents and staff is essential.

A school's anti-bullying policy needs to be readily available and clear about the steps school will take when bullying is reported.

g. Consider seating plans

Teachers, rather than pupils, choose where pupils should sit. Pupils are placed in the classroom considering specific needs and accommodations (informed by student passports and profiles).

h. Have trusted people to turn to

Gareth uses the term 'corporate responsibility' in relation to whole-school provision, meaning that at every level of the school a variety of adults and peers can be approached. Pupils should be able to identify a handful of individuals they can confide in safely.

WHAT TO DO IF YOU SUSPECT YOUR CHILD IS BEING BULLIED

As a parent, the first thing you can do to help your child overcome any bullying is to create an environment in which they are likely to share any worries with you. So...

1. Keep in touch with your teen

If you have a nightly chat, even a 15-minute one, you can keep an eye on your child's state of mind and spot any subtle changes. If you're just 'there', there's a chance something might be mentioned that otherwise wouldn't be until it got to crisis point.

This doesn't mean asking lots of questions; simply being present and attentive is all that it takes. Rather than interviewing your child, just keep them company for a little while, showing an interest in their interests.

2. Encourage worry discussion

Worry boxes can be a good strategy for storing anxieties from the day that can be shared later. You can have an imaginary 'worry box' where worries stay under lock and key until they can be discussed, or a real one (better for autistic kids) where notelets are kept and selected in turn with a parent.

3. Be mindful of their reaction

Keeping calm when a child tells you something upsetting about their day is important. Autistic children tend to be nervous of huge reactions, and if they feel that you may do something that is outside of their control, they'll be less likely to open up to you.

From school's perspective, according to Gareth, it would always be preferable to share information early, even if there was an agreement for no direct action at that stage. This is where positive relationships are so important, as 'small' things can often grow rapidly when unchecked.

4. Collaborate on a plan

Collaboration puts your teenager in the driving seat rather than feeling that the situation is freewheeling out of their control. So, if nothing is done immediately, maybe they'd like to monitor the situation and report back after a week.

5. Alert school early and keep a log

It's far better to allow school to nip a situation in the bud than to wait until a situation is causing your child daily anxiety. By chatting to your child regularly about their day, and maybe offering anecdotes from your own secondary school days, you may be able to get early warning of signs that a peer is becoming problematic. Ask school to keep a situation on their radar (even if your child wants nothing done at this point) and watch for interactions.

6. Keep in regular touch with school

Rather than waiting for an update, ask for a quick chat each week on whether the bullying situation is improving. If possible, as we always say, a face-to-face talk is preferable and will ensure that school can discuss strategies with you.

For more information on bullying and help in combatting it, please see the specialist websites we've included for this chapter in Appendix 2: References and Resources.

CHAPTER 10

MAKING FRIENDS

Inclusive schools recognise that friendships can be difficult for autistic pupils and they have systems that will support building relationships with peers.

However, don't feel too dismayed if your son or daughter isn't making friends quickly and easily.

Debby remembers that within the first fortnight of her son joining secondary school, she asked him if he'd met anyone he liked yet.

'Not yet, I'm just trying to survive right now,' he reported.

What he meant was friendships weren't part of settling in for him. They were the 'icing on the cake' when his system had accommodated all the other changes in the environment.

There is a tendency towards a different set of priorities compared with other children – who will perhaps see friendships as the most important aspect of settling in and seek them out at the first opportunity – and no wonder, when there are so many other challenges for autistic pupils to overcome in a new environment.

The second thing to bear in mind is that it shouldn't feel surprising that autistic children don't find as many people with whom they can instantly bond as their classmates. This isn't due to lack of likeability!

If your child has specific interests, or 'specialisms' as we like to call them, conversations outside those interests can be pretty hard work. They involve processing new information rather than familiar material. Remember Alfie Bowen's recollections about 'learning' others' interests? It just wasn't natural for him.

During the demands of a day at school, this means that the friendships that will be easiest for your child are likely to be with those teens who share the same interests. The chat will be familiar and easier to process. So...it follows that your child's pool of potential friendship candidates can be a little smaller as a result!

This doesn't mean that they won't be able to make friendships at school. It does suggest, however, that you shouldn't be surprised if they don't immediately find like-minded souls.

So, what can you do to help?

SCHOOLS CAN...
1. Establish clubs and activities

A good way for schools to support young people during unstructured break and lunch times is to establish clubs and activities based on the interests of their pupils.

For example, as we mentioned earlier, many of the students at one school enjoyed Manga (Japanese comics and graphic novels in a particular style). School staff purposely set up activities and a club around that and allowed non-autistic peers to join as well.

This can be a fantastic way for pupils to connect with each other and can be hugely powerful.

In the same setting, other students enjoyed a gym club that was run by one of the site management team; the structure of the club along with the physical nature of it was popular with many students who found the lack of structure at lunchtime difficult.

Ensuring there were clear, planned times for lunch before or after the club enabled a very positive experience for everyone.

2. Be mindful of seating plans

Teachers can also bear in mind that seating plans and the way teaching is structured offer opportunities to support autistic students socially. They can work with autistic students to consider auditory distractions, but also place them near to potential friends, for example.

A parent told us she emailed one teacher to let him know that her son was feeling a bit isolated. 'Great seating plan because it's nice and quiet,' she commented. 'Unfortunately, he never talks to anyone. Is there anything you can do?'

This is such a great example of solving problems through great collaboration. Taking into account practicalities that she couldn't herself see, she left the ball in the teacher's court. He rose to the challenge immediately, finding a place near to a peer who was showing signs of potential friendship, but still maintaining distance from the nosier elements in the class.

This may not always be possible, but early discussions can make it into a *possibility*.

PARENTS CAN...

1. Develop social skills (in collaboration with school)

Writing about improving social skills is always tricky. We run the risk of suggesting that your autistic child isn't 'good enough' until they learn a neurotypical/non-autistic way of conversing. And that's by no means the message that we want to give.

However, there's a lot to be said for helping autistic children to be aware of others' points of view. What you don't know naturally, it's possible to learn in a comfortable environment.

So, when you're having a chat at home, instead of glazing over as your autistic child talks about their special interest, do them a favour and listen to them in the same way that anyone else would.

Explain to them Debby's favourite little concept of 'listening patience' – that people can only listen to a conversation without joining in for about two minutes before their ears start to get a bit tired.

These kinds of 'rules of thumb' make it a lot easier for autistic people to navigate confusing unspoken social rules, and in turn can make them feel confident and calmer around others.

Debby used to have chats about Pokémon with her son. Rather than saving 'special interest talk' for certain times (a completely unrealistic way of socialising), they'd have a chat at any time, and Bobby would learn to explain something from the beginning, pause, ask questions and check for understanding and opinions.

Debby focuses in quite some detail on helping children understand others' thoughts in her book *Fifteen Things They Forgot to Tell You About Autism* (Chapter 11: 'You Can Learn What You Lack').

Remember, you aren't fundamentally trying to change an autistic person or force them to pretend to be non-autistic. That way lies trouble.

You are simply developing skills so that they're able to meet non-autistic people halfway during interactions, and with a bit of patience and understanding, neurotypicals can do the same. It's just developing an understanding that will stand them in good stead in all future interactions.

Whether your child is chatting online on a gaming or hobby forum, or talking to their cousins, once they get the opportunity to fine-tune their conversation skills, they'll start to improve them. This is why it's important to...

2. Encourage other outlets, rather than just classmates

In order to prevent isolation, don't just limit finding friendships to within school. Find groups that focus on your child's interests.

Don't rule out online friendships. These can be as meaningful and crucial to an autistic child's wellbeing as a friendship made in 'real life'. Many parents are suspicious of these types of friendships, and with online dangers you have every right to be cautious, but don't rule out well-managed sites or forums with good monitoring.

> I believe that the best way to make friends as an autistic is through special interests. At least, that's how I did it. When I was younger, I was Disneyland obsessed. I joined a message board and was on there almost every day. On the board, people wrote trip reports and discussed new and existing rides. I don't think I met any of those people in real life, but I also had a blog on which I posted my adventures, and through that I met my ex-boyfriend.
>
> *Bianca Toeps,* AuKids *magazine, Issue 50, January 2021*

In fact, friendships online can be great for autistic children, as they take away the stresses of reading body language and any environmental distractions.

For this reason, one thing you can do to benefit your child is to ensure you're both up to speed with online safety knowledge. We've added some links you can follow up in Appendix 2: References and Resources, including a link to an article in *AuKids* magazine Issue 21, which you can download for free and has full internet safety guidance.

Something we can recommend for Minecraft fans is Autcraft (www. autcraft.com), a Minecraft server built by dad Stuart Duncan, which is especially for autistic youngsters. It feels no different to the ordinary Minecraft game but is safer and has great systems in place to look after its players. Spectrum Gaming (www.spectrumgaming.net) is another safe online place run by and for autistic people.

Fact: The younger generation has more contact with people online than previous generations. It isn't enough just to shake your head and say 'that's not a proper way of making friends'. For them *it is* and for this reason their training and yours in internet safety is important.

3. Teach the balance model

Friendships incorporate a multitude of subtle signals. To avoid having to interpret them all, you can teach your child some 'rules of thumb'.

Help them to recognise what the 'balance' of a good friendship looks like.

a. Balance of shared conversation

Imagine a set of old-fashioned weighing scales (if you have some, so much the better!).

When a friendship is balanced, both people get a chance to talk. A simple rule of thumb is to say that people can talk for about two minutes non-stop before the other person runs out of 'listening patience'. Then it's their turn to speak. You might be able to chat for longer on what interests you by asking them questions as you go along, which gives them a turn to talk. What do they think of what you've said? Do they agree? What's their view? After a question, they should leave a pause to give the other person time to think.

Are they worried that they might forget to tell their friend something?

A great line to remember is: 'Oh! I don't want to interrupt you but remind me to tell you about...'

Use home as practice ground. It's perfectly natural to glaze over and nod dumbly after a 15-minute soliloquy. Some parents do this because they don't want to offend their youngster.

However, fine-tune those friendship skills by practising the art of 'listening patience' with them. Listen as a friend may do, and if they don't fully explain something new, explain your confusion:

> I don't really know enough about that subject to understand what you are saying there. Can you explain that to me?

There will be times when you don't have the energy to do this, and that's fine. But spending a proportion of your time together practising those skills without your child really being aware will do them a surprising amount of good.

Sometimes autistic youngsters talk a lot because they are afraid of having to process new auditory information at a pace that they won't understand or remember. So, show your youngster what they can say when they don't understand or when they need thinking time.

Sorry, can I just interrupt you for a second? What does that word mean again?

Could you just repeat that?

I didn't quite understand that bit. Could you phrase it another way? My literal brain is finding that hard!

Hmm, not sure about that question. Can I think about it?

It's helpful to show autistic kids that they don't have to be passive during listening. In fact, people will appreciate that they've made an effort to listen properly by asking for clarification.

Give them the power to explain what their difficulties are and take ownership of their own interactions without having to opt out of them altogether.

Having taught these skills to Bobby, Debby was happy to observe that when he was at the dentist recently and paused while she was asking him something, he said, 'Sorry, that's just a bit of my OCD.' He didn't need to explain, as it was a specialist dentist, but he'd learnt that it's okay to make a conversation smoother by openly saying where there's difficulty.

> *Give them the power to explain what their difficulties are and take ownership of their own interactions without having to opt out of them altogether.*

It can take the pressure off to explain that no one needs to remember every bit of information they're given or even understand everything

– just being attentive and listening is enough. Let's take you, for example. Can you remember everything a friend told you about themselves on your last meeting? Bet you can't! You knew that it was enough to be interested and attentive, and to remember the important facts. Does your child realise this, or do they feel that because someone has told them something, they are duty-bound to hold it in their heads?

Let's not assume what their perception might be and the awful pressure our young people can put on themselves.

b. Balance of effort

Who is putting the effort into this friendship? Is your teenager always the one who texts? Have a chat about the balance here.

Explain to your child that just as they can get overwhelmed by noise in a busy classroom, friends can become overwhelmed by too much attention or demands on their time. Those friends will hardly ever tell you when your attention is too much for them, because they don't want to hurt your feelings.

Talk about the differences between people: that one person won't mind you being around them or texting them a lot, but another will mind very much. Therefore, you have to be guided by them, and find a balance by replying to them when they text you back, rather than starting a lot of conversations that go unanswered. When explaining this to my son, we called this matching someone's 'friendship style', recounts Debby.

Matching the effort that the other person puts into the friendship is the key to getting a balance. If your child is making all the effort and their friend is making none, it's worth a chat about the friendship.

c. Balance of respect

Is this friend as kind to you as you are to them? How do they return your kindness? Do they lend you games, invite you over, listen when you're feeling down? Do they talk to you without using unkind language?

If you have an old set of weighing scales, you can physically show the balance model using them. Put a weight on one side, showing that their friend has put 'weight' into the friendship by texting them or asking them to play, and then a weight on the other side, showing that your child has contacted them back. You can use an established friendship to demonstrate this.

Then show what happens when one person makes all the effort – the friendship becomes unbalanced. The trouble with an unbalanced friendship is that it is unlikely to last, because it is unequal.

That suggests that your child may be overwhelming their friend, or they may be making all the effort. Even if we don't mind making slightly more effort, people who won't balance the scales at all with their own efforts aren't being real friends.

When a friendship starts but doesn't last, it's usually because it's unbalanced.

Using physical examples like the scales really helps explain these difficult abstract concepts.

We don't want autistic adults to be the only ones making a huge effort socially. We want them to be treated with dignity and respect. In order for this to happen, they need to understand the rules of balance as children. A friend who makes no effort is no friend at all, and shouldn't be treated as one.

4. Keeping friends

For some kids, other people can become just another 'special interest' and it's hard to learn that they have needs and motivations of their own.

But giving your child certain things to listen for can work – such as making it a 'mission' to find out the three things that their friend is most interested in. Now, don't expect them to learn in any depth about areas that are of no interest to them! However, realising that your own interests aren't the same as everyone else's can be key to developing fresh perspectives.

We'd also recommend that the focus when a child meets up with a friend isn't on 'playing together' but on 'doing together'. This gives both friends something to concentrate on other than social interactions.

So don't worry if gaming is the focus – they're building their social skills as they play!

5. Body language awareness

There's a danger here that by showing autistic children how to use positive body language, you might be trying to work against the grain of what is natural for them. As Debby said in an article for *AuKids* magazine:

> I'm often mindful that the 'fake it till you make it' school of socialising, often practised expertly by autistic girls, puts a tremendous strain on a person. Not only that, but it causes others to demand more of them than they may be capable of giving.

'Smile Like You Mean It', AuKids *magazine, Issue 46*

Having said that, information is power. Nothing can be lost by explaining why people might make assumptions based on body language. For instance, if you never smile on greeting someone, it does help to know that they may assume you aren't pleased to see them. This is discussed more fully in the article mentioned, which is included in Appendix 2: References and Resources.

6. Don't worry!

Some children are more bothered than others about making friends. If your child is struggling, however, it can be upsetting for you and anxiety-provoking for them.

Do reinforce to your child that they are likeable and brilliant and worth knowing, but that they just haven't found their tribe yet! If you are calm about it, the chances are they will feel much better, too.

CHAPTER 11

WHEN CONFLICT IS ON THE HORIZON

Before approaching a potential conflict with school, we have some advice for parents.

1. BE CLEAR OF THE REAL PROBLEM

If your child is in opposition to something being imposed on them at school, the understandable reaction is to take their argument to the school and champion their views. After all, they are autistic and reasonable adjustments must be made.

However, try to adopt a questioning attitude and examine the problem as much as you can from all sides until you decide on the right stance to take. There are definite advantages in taking time to reflect, think and take stock here, if the circumstances allow.

We can be nervous of pushing our own children, but ask yourself some questions. For instance, in the case of a proposed change, is the difficulty the change itself, or is your child anxious because of the way it's being introduced?

What is the purpose of this change, seen from both your child's viewpoint and the school's – and could it benefit them?

Could you suggest a more successful approach if school's is causing anxiety and stress? Maybe a staged approach with a clearly defined roadmap would be a positive way forward?

Although it's important to trust your child's feelings, try to look a little deeper into the meanings behind the words they are using.

The word 'no' can mean more than one thing, and in the case of autistic children it's often linked to difficulty being flexible, as we're sure you're aware:

I don't like change, I'm comfortable with things how they are.
I don't know exactly what to expect.
What happens if I don't like this change? Can I go back?
What if I do this and I can't control my feelings and get a 'meltdown'?

'No' is a convenient default position for some autistic youngsters, especially when they can't see any particular benefit to saying 'yes', and change can mean uncertainty. Remember our quote from Alis Rowe? 'I do not like to confirm things because then the thing becomes a reality. The reality tends to involve a lot of effort, and always involves a large amount of anxiety.'

What can you do?

Imagine that you are shown a small room and then someone locks the door behind you. Rather than looking at the room itself, you'll focus on the fact that there's no escape from it.

This is what change can feel like to autistic children.

So, when changes are made at school, rather than rejecting them outright because your child doesn't like them, consider each change on its own merits, and, most importantly, how to explain and support understanding of the change – simply being told about something verbally in an assembly, for example, is not likely to be most effective.

And if the change might actually benefit your child, encourage school to show them an escape route. This means adequate preparation, helping the pupil know exactly what to expect and showing them a way out as a Plan B if they struggle to cope.

Help school to introduce change by:

- Talking to the child about the benefits of the change, if that's the case.
- Asking the youngster what benefits they can think of when doing things in this new way. As with any change, work as a democracy – exchange thoughts.
- Gather the nature of their anxieties and stressors. When they say 'no', what objections are they really raising?

Then structure the change in such a way that an escape route is visible.

- The change should be introduced slowly and gradually.
- Their feelings should be monitored as the change progresses.
- After a set length of time, the change should be reviewed.
- If unsuccessful, the change should be reconsidered or adapted.
- If an 'escape plan' is given (i.e. try it and if you still don't like it, you can leave) – it should be honoured to ensure trust and future cooperation.

The last point in the box is a *really* important one. If you agree a plan, stick to it! Changing or denying access to support or an agreed pathway is difficult for everyone, but particularly an autistic person, and a negative experience here will erode their trust in school, making them more resistant to change in the future.

By giving these fallback options, you reduce anxiety and therefore increase flexibility.

So, turn a 'no' into an 'I'll try it' or 'maybe' by showing this escape route. And when they do say 'I'll try it' or 'maybe', don't forget to praise like crazy for their brilliant flexibility, recognising that change is difficult and that wow! they've overcome it. (When we say 'praise like crazy', obviously adapt this for your child's tolerance of noisy praise!)

Small regular changes can be very good for increasing overall flexibility; however, they need to be done in an environment that already feels safe and comfortable. That's why Chapter 5 on comforts is so important, and why choosing a school that gives them 'background calm' and consistency is also so very important. Not only can we not learn when we are stressed, but nor can we adapt. Possibly one of the biggest gifts you can give your child is the ability to be a little more adaptable, recognising that this a key difficulty for them and so there's a need to tread carefully.

By the way, there are things you can do at home to encourage flexibility, as Debby points out in her earlier book *Fifteen Things They Forgot to Tell You About Autism* (2018). Another book by Lauren Kerstein is terrific in this respect – *A Week of Switching, Shifting, and Stretching: How to Make My Thinking More Flexible* (2014). If you don't want to commit to that just yet, have a look at the free to download article in Issue 33 of *AuKids* magazine, 'From a Black and White World to Thinking in Colour – How to improve flexibility of thought.' We'll include both in Appendix 2: References and Resources for this chapter.

People under threat are less flexible. That's the same whether or not you're autistic. Survival comes first – that is a human response.

2. TRANSLATE ACCURATELY: SEPARATE ONE PROBLEM FROM ANOTHER

Anxiety can make kids bundle up many issues together, and so it's important when examining their resistance or fear to uncover the precise source of anxiety and to agree with your child the priorities for 'fixing' issues. If they struggle with this, we like to use the 'magic wand' question.

> If you could wave a magic wand, what would be the first thing that would change about school tomorrow?

As autistic people tend to deal with concretes more easily than abstracts, it's sometimes a good idea to rate problems on a scale of 1–10, talking through why they've given them each score. In this way, you might see that if you solve one issue, the others will immediately follow.

For instance, in one case, a young man was uneasy about leaving lessons on time and needed to have a buddy with him to do so. School then tried to abruptly stop the buddy system. Well, where to start? They hadn't unwrapped the real cause of the problem, which was *not* simply noisy corridors but also the potential for bullying from older pupils during transition times. The youngster was very logically thinking *safety in numbers*. Therefore, when school tried to stop the buddy system, they were removing his sense of safety.

The real problem was not that he needed a buddy; if the school culture had been safer, he would have been okay leaving lessons early on his own, to avoid the disruption and noise of busy corridors. And, as Gareth has stated elsewhere, there are whole-school procedures and policies that can be put in place to make transition times less chaotic anyway – starting with doing away with the bell! (Didn't we notice everyone has watches these days?!)

The real purpose of chatting with your child about their resistance to change is to help school get to the bottom of what's really troubling them and put in strategies that get to the heart of the matter, rather than act as a sticking plaster.

Obviously in this case, culture was an issue, but another was a mis-diagnosis of the problem. If this keeps happening, and school refuses to listen to your reasoning, then we're on to the next few chapters. But not yet...

3. PREPARE YOUR CHILD FOR COMPROMISE

Sometimes solving a problem doesn't mean perfection, depending on the practicalities involved. Would a compromise work? For this reason, it's a great idea to teach autistic children what the word 'compromise' means. You can do this in quite a scientific way by writing down the issue from both viewpoints, with the critical factors on each side, and showing possible compromises to consider.

The best way of preparing kids for compromise is to try it at home with smaller decisions as they arise (rather than hypothetically), where the compromise won't bother them much. That way they get used to the concept.

For instance...

You want Weetabix today, but the problem is if you have two pieces of Weetabix, there won't be enough for your brother. What's a good compromise?

You want to go to the park, but Mum needs some things from the shop before tomorrow. What's a good compromise?

You probably don't realise it, but you are constantly teaching your child the art of compromise – so explain what the word means as you're doing this, and how great it is to be able to be flexible enough to reach one.

As this involves thinking through a problem from another's view-point, compromise can be extremely challenging for an autistic person, but it is a skill for life if they can start to see that any problem they experience at school is multifaceted.

4. DISCUSS THE APPROACH

We hope that small difficulties can be easily solved without you needing to visit school. If your child is very clear on who to approach for help and when, and you've helped them to identify the precise obstacle they are facing, let's hope that things can be resolved without your input. After all, learning to problem-solve in this way is just brilliant independence for your youngster.

So, if you were very accustomed to picking up the phone when they were at primary school, just wait a second. Ask yourself the question that's a must for all parents at some time or other:

Can my youngster actually sort this out on their own with a bit of support from me?

They may not have been able to do this when they were six or seven, but things may well have moved on since then!

Your child may be confiding in you because they are building up to saying something themselves, and just need your help in finding the right people to approach, words to say and place to have the conversation. If so, that's incredibly mature and they deserve praise for it. Thinking things through with you and writing some key thoughts will help.

Assuming that the issue is more complex and you feel that adult input is needed, should you ask your child's permission before you discuss an issue with school? Absolutely. You may be thinking along the lines of 'I'll handle this' – indeed, that's the way you may be used to. But your child is growing and developing, and, as part of that, needs to have an insight into how successful resolutions are achieved and be part of the decision-making.

Your child may be nervous about the thought of you broaching an issue. It's good to make it clear that if you chat, it won't be a conflict, but it's simply to explain anything that's unclear, and to try to find a way to solve problems together. As preparation for that chat, you're gathering all the information you can. Making the youngster part of that preparation and asking them for information will not only help them to feel in control but ensure that you have a full picture.

What if they don't want you to say anything? In the interests of trust and respect, you need to honour their wishes, but you can point out that it's very difficult to change things for the better unless you have communication with school. Present this as a positive thing; you've always worked with their school and this is just an extension of your regular catch-ups. It's yet another reason why regular chats with school staff in good times makes any approach so much easier. Your youngster is used to the relationship and it's not a big deal when a parent sets foot inside the school gates.

5. AVOID EMAILING AN ESSAY

So, you've decided that something needs to be discussed with school. If you write to say you would like a meeting, we'd advise you to limit the pre-meeting email to a brief outline of the reason for the meeting.

What can sometimes happen is that you write down a lot of information, school responds in kind, and before you know it, you've got the kind of conversation that should have been saved for the meeting. This isn't really ideal, as a lot can get missed and, as we've said earlier in the book, meeting in person is always best before tensions rise further.

6. DON'T SET YOURSELF UP FOR CONFLICT

When a difficulty comes along, don't assume that 'someone has got it wrong'.

We've heard more than once this sort of fighting talk:

> Someone's got it wrong and when I find out who it is they're going to regret it.

Actually, there are many factors that can influence these situations (particularly unintended consequences of policies developed away from those who know learners with additional needs well), so let's consider taking a broader approach when tackling difficulties.

Schools rely on great communication to ensure that everyone

adopts the right strategies with your child. If information didn't filter through to an individual, it isn't necessarily their fault if they misjudge a situation.

Rather than making someone pay for their misunderstanding, plan to ensure that they understand what went wrong and why – and, most importantly, reflect and change things for the future.

CHAPTER 12

HANDLING DISAGREEMENTS

So…how to handle that tricky situation when misunderstandings have occurred and things look like they might turn nasty.

When people talk about handling 'challenging' behaviour in autistic children (a term we don't much like, as I think we more than made clear earlier!), some refer to 'escalation'.

Escalation is a handy way of considering what also happens when a misunderstanding occurs between education staff and carers.

Escalation happens when a lack of understanding between two parties creates a build-up of emotion until there is a complete breakdown in communication.

When it comes to the carer–teacher relationship, you can prevent escalation. You may not be able to escape disagreement, but we believe you can escape conflict. As Gareth often says: 'You can disagree with people without being difficult or antagonistic.' Who benefits from that? Certainly not the young person.

Why would you want to escape conflict if conflict gets you what you want?

In the short term, conflict could be successful in getting you action. Indeed, you may have learnt through experience that those who shout loudest get what they want more often than those who are less...er... forthright.

It's a shame that this is the experience of many parents, leading to much unnecessary antagonism and lasting mistrust.

By all means, keep 'shout louder' in your toolbox as a back-up. However, we'd advise against using it as your default stance.

The trouble is that getting what you want at the expense of the other party's 'buy-in' and agreement means that, in the long term, you're setting yourself up for further conflict, further misunderstandings, plus a fight every time you want something.

On the other hand, successful collaboration means that you generate understanding, which leads to problems becoming easier and easier to solve, rather than harder and harder.

Problems that are solved with a deep understanding of *why* an approach is being taken are more likely to be solved *well*.

So, our first recommendation is for both parents and staff to avoid Blazing Keyboard Syndrome.

Blazing Keyboard Syndrome is a very well-recognised knee-jerk reaction to your child being upset.

It's hugely understandable, and to be honest, everyone has been there at some point in the past.

Your child comes home in tears because of something that's happened at school. In the old days, when we were cavemen, you'd grab the nearest wooden club, shout 'Og!' and off you'd go to sort it out in a physical kind of way. Your offspring has been threatened, and in 'lower-brain' terms, that's one heck of a trigger.

> *Your child comes home in tears because of something that's happened at school. In the old days, when we were cavemen, you'd grab the nearest wooden club, shout 'Og!' and off you'd go to sort it out in a physical kind of way. Your offspring has been threatened, and in 'lower-brain' terms, that's one heck of a trigger.*

Although we've evolved somewhat, we have the same prehistoric lower-brain reaction when threatened nowadays. Instead of using a club, however, you are more inclined to boot up the computer and set its keyboard alight.

The angrier we get, the more formal and spikey our language becomes, as we wield legal swords over education heads. The most used phrase for the parent keyboard warrior is 'reasonable adjustments'. The trouble is, because the equality law (Equality Act 2010) was designed for more than just autistic folks, it is a bit on the hazy side as to what is deemed a reasonable adjustment. Therefore, they only seem reasonable if your school is, too.

Blazing Keyboard Syndrome is sometimes met with equal fierceness (albeit daubed in fairly formal speak from the school) and before we know it, we're into a war of words and entrenched attitudes.

Communication here is only going to be one way, and that might be just the way you want it when in a state of high emotion.

We suggest that at this point you breathe, have a coffee (herbal tea, chai latte, whatever...), take a step back, gather the facts and then write an email, or make a phone call, asking for a face-to-face chat.

By the way, a common method of 'resolving' disputes is by first setting the keyboard alight with an angry or passive-aggressive exchange and *then* going in for a chat.

That's not quite what we meant.

If you do that, honest discussion and collaboration can't take place at any meeting that follows, because the other party is too busy trying to keep a professional lid on the emotional carnage you've unleashed in them personally.

Parents: We're not saying that there won't be people reading this whose children have had a rough time because of some ignorant people. Believe us, we have heard it all.

Go in. See them. Or (if you must) hold a virtual meeting. It's possible you can head off direct confrontation, but you need to admit to yourself that you're dealing with human beings. All human beings make mistakes, and if you treat people with respect, you're giving them a better chance of rectifying them than if you attack them.

Teachers: Don't be tempted to respond to e-mails written during attacks of Blazing Keyboard Syndrome when a parent is in a high state of emotion. Pulling apart their arguments in a point-by-point defence isn't going to calm down anyone (well okay, it may make *you* feel better).

Suggest that there are serious concerns raised and it would be a good idea to chat face to face. Please don't delay with a meeting. The longer an angry parent waits unanswered, the angrier they'll feel.

This leads us on to the much-overlooked vehicle for any change to your child's education.

THE MEETING

We show up, we share our views, we leave. What's to talk about?

We may never consciously perceive 'the meeting' as something that we need to analyse in any detail.

However, whether or not you achieve decent collaboration – for now and in the future – depends on how both parents and education staff approach meetings, whether these are quick catch-ups, annual reviews or those difficult discussions we all know and dread.

Your number-one barrier either as a parent or as a teacher is being unaware of your own method of engagement and its impact on a meeting.

Be aware that your collaboration with someone can't move forward if you've inwardly already given them a label. This goes for both sides. Sometimes when we don't know people outside a meeting room, we can get quite good at labelling them.

Debby doesn't wish to stereotype here, but it's also worth noting that if you're a mum, we do tend to chat to each other about school, and when we chat about professionals whom our friends don't know, these labels are spoken out loud, and become uncompromising as a result. It's very rare we'll change our minds and say:

You know I said that guy was useless? Well, actually he's not.

Do you recognise describing professionals with these labels?

She's woolly.
He's completely insensitive.
That one never listens.
She's basically a cow.
He's utterly ineffective.

Or teachers, do you recognise these labels?

She's a moaner, never happy.
That one never listens.
The apple hasn't dropped far from the tree, there.

These labels will naturally inform how you approach someone, and most are pretty horrible and based on judgements made from previous prejudices – in essence, rarely does this offer anything positive regarding solutions.

Don't give up on a person. A collaboration is down to you both working with each other's strengths and shortcomings. Allow them to move outside your earlier label.

★ If you feel she's woolly, be prepared to ask questions until you get to definite answers.

★ If you feel that he is often insensitive, perhaps you could more openly state what you are feeling and why.

★ If you don't feel that they listen, the collaborative approaches stated later in this chapter will ensure that they will!

★ Maybe someone was ineffective last time you spoke to them. Maybe they had a bad day or were feeling slightly threatened by your approach.

Try to approach each meeting as a fresh chance to collaborate more effectively this time.

The more you 'paint' a person as an adversary, the more they will become one, responding to your approach.

So, be slow to judge.

The more you encourage open dialogue as a parent, the more you'll get to see what's really happening on the other side of the fence. Staff are more likely to be open with you about other pressures that they're under and how this may understandably influence their practices.

This isn't to say that you must accept the unacceptable, but it does give you a better starting point from which to recover that relationship and move forward.

The best kind of teaching practice is reflective practice; staff 'own their own fragility' (Gareth's favourite phrase) and consider what they could have done differently. They're not able to do that if they feel they are being attacked.

In addition to this, consider your style of engagement and your own emotions.

You might approach meetings as the **king or queen of jargon**. Well read and well clued up. Using jargon has helped you to be respected in the past, but it doesn't necessarily make for successful collaboration as it can just feel like one-upmanship. Plus, when one person understands jargon and another doesn't, a lot gets lost in translation. As well as that, you may both be using a term and each have a different understanding of it.

Are you a **fighter**? You may not admit it to yourself, but you go to meetings aiming to win. Stridently expressing your views gets you heard – but it doesn't mean that you are understood. Successful long-term change is forged by being understood, rather than simply being heard.

If you're a **smoother**, you may want as little aggravation as possible and to avoid any conflict. But your tendencies to keep everyone happy may mean that you end up agreeing to something that doesn't really convince you.

So, before the meeting, be aware of:

★ your labels and assumptions and

★ your engagement styles.

If you want to truly collaborate, you need to treat each situation as a blank canvas.

Here are eight easy ways in which parents and education staff can give themselves the best chance of successful collaboration.

1. Be clear on goals

Both sides need to be clear what this meeting is for, gather information beforehand and be clear what you want to leave with. Make notes on what you'd like to ask and, if possible, maybe a friend or relative can come to make notes for you during the discussions so you can concentrate fully.

Be mindful of the amount of time you'll have and consider top priorities. It is always good to clarify the timeframe of a meeting at the start – knowing timings helps massively with framing key points. Ensure that everyone is aware of the full background beforehand to prevent you losing precious time by going over old ground.

2. Check others' views as you go

Every time a point is made, check reactions around the table.

What's your take on that?

Is that your understanding as well?

Are you okay with that?

Asking for other people's views is central to collaboration. If a teacher has contributed their own ideas and thoughts to a meeting, they are more likely to put the resulting suggestions into practice. They are not simply listened to; they are *heard*.

If you feel you'll burst if you don't 'get it said', write down key points beforehand.

3. Agree on common ground

If it feels that someone is on the wrong track, backtrack until you can agree common ground.

The common ground is what has been observed – the undeniable facts. It's the starting point of any solution.

Summarise the common ground and your understanding of both perspectives on it. Check your understanding is right. This prevents people from talking over each other because they aren't feeling heard.

Bingo. You're into the territory where you can talk about autism, how it seems to some people and what's really causing reactions. Then you can reach a solution together.

- ★ Do staff understand that resistance to change in autistic people is caused by inflexibility of thought, and that it's a key difficulty for autistic people?

- ★ Do they understand the causes of overload?

Have a look at our Chapters 6 and 7 addressing some of these barriers and consider the true reasons for the responses that are being observed.

It's always best to recognise that many responses are caused by an overactive fight-or-flight response in autism. Most people recognise that fight or flight is part of our natural survival instinct and instantly 'get' that kind of language so it becomes very useful.

In AuKids' autism training, Debby and her colleague Tori Houghton use a cartoon of two cavemen to illustrate freeze, fight or flight in autism. One of them is frozen on the spot in front of a sabre tooth tiger; the other is running away.

We then talk about what sorts of responses you would observe in autism that are equivalent to this. Avoidance strategies to cope with a threatening environment include blocking your ears, covering your eyes, making your own noise or running. That's the equivalent of flight. If you're shutting down and being unresponsive, that's freeze. And if you're rude or disruptive, that's fight.

These are ancient instincts caused by a nervous system on red alert. So, encourage professionals not to focus on the rude of disruptive, but to take away the sabre tooth tiger!

It's worth noting here that 'flight' is often the first port of call – those coping mechanisms that allow for escape. Aggression usually follows when the first avenue is blocked. If a child is cornered and unable to escape a situation, things might take a turn for the worse. So your job is in negotiating either prevention (take away the sabre tooth tiger – the best solution) or a form of escape.

When you express your own views, talk about your observations, followed by what you believe is happening as a result.

Sometimes as a parent, it helps to fully accept that there can be alternative ways of seeing things and that your child isn't perfect! This ensures that you look balanced.

Couple of hints here... First, accept someone else's version of reality as valid. Second, admit that it's a possibility – don't throw out their view because you don't agree with it. Third, prepare them with the idea that you'd like to delve a bit deeper into motivations, and ask them if they wouldn't mind hearing those thoughts, rather than diving straight in with them.

This way, if you've made an inaccurate observation, that misunderstanding can be addressed.

4. Agree on the solution before you agree on the method

You can spend quite a while disagreeing on the way to go about achieving something, but it pays first to agree on what you'd like to achieve.

For example:

So, we've agreed that we need to find a way of avoiding overload at this time because when it happens it's really disruptive to her and to everyone else.

So, we've agreed that we need to find a way to avoid these kinds of confrontations, caused by his perception of pressure, and then he'd focus better in class.

5. Use neutral language

Meetings where blame is being laid at someone's feet don't usually get very far. Defensive people can't collaborate; they are too busy holding up a virtual shield to deflect your offending words. Talk about 'situations' and focus on what would help going forward, rather than what has hindered.

So, in future, what can we do to avoid the situation where he feels under attack and runs off?

Notice in this description that the parent hasn't kept it to observed behaviour, but includes the reason for it, too. It's not the behaviour we want to eradicate ('Stop running!') but the cause of distress (he feels under attack).

Here's where the stress support plan mentioned earlier by Gareth can really help a team to refocus on a solution-focused approach to a situation.

6. Keep it real: Talk about feelings

So many conversations end up stilted because we are in a 'meeting'. But if you have strong emotions that are governing your reactions and approach, you need to bravely state what those emotions are. Expressing emotions openly stops those feelings from 'leaking' out during a meeting, being hinted at but never being addressed. This isn't weak; it's keeping the focus on what matters. Sometimes people need to understand how it feels to have a youngster crying to them in the evening because they feel they've been treated unjustly. Having a child who dreads attending school is the worst feeling in the world. Sometimes, it helps to have that picture painted as a focus for positive change.

7. Sum up

At the end of the meeting, sum up what's been agreed – who is doing what and by when. If you're a parent, you could ask for a summary of the meeting; it focuses both sides on action. As a SENCo, Gareth always agreed to send the bullet points of actions afterwards – just who is doing what and by when, along with the agreed follow-up meeting – clear, concise and with the opportunity for a reply or amendment if something is missed or incorrect. Agree a follow-up meeting date to check on progress. Don't leave feeling short-changed.

8. Focus on positives

The fact that people are prepared to meet and discuss issues is a good thing. Keep everyone buoyant by thanking them for coming and saying that you appreciate their input. Gratitude goes such a long way. Appreciating the efforts that are going into solving difficulties leaves people with a positive energy that translates into action.

WHAT CAN GO WRONG IN MEETINGS?
1. Power Battle Part 1

Someone assumed that you knew less about autism than you did and spoke to you as if you had the brains of a small newt. It got your back up and you became hostile. After that, views were aired, but the relationship took a turn for the worse.

Solution: Try to avoid being defensive and jumping in with 'YES, I KNOW ALL THAT!' tempting as it may be. Do quietly say something like:

Thanks, I'm aware of those difficulties. Do you feel there's anything I've misunderstood here?

In other words, reframe the conversation. Are they explaining because they feel as if you don't 'get it' or have they simply assumed less knowledge than you have?

2. Power Battle Part 2

You had a great time beguiling people with your superior knowledge, but are they totally convinced by your arguments? Now that you think about it, you're not entirely sure.

If you do have good knowledge, that *will* come across; you don't have to lamp people over the head with it.

Keep collaboration at centre stage. Share your views and check responses to them – make this constant throughout the meeting.

3. Someone says something you blatantly disagree with

The temptation is to respond: 'No, no, no, no. That's rubbish'.

A more successful response might be:

Let me understand why you think that...

Once they've supplied their logic, you can follow it up:

Ah, now I understand why you feel that way. Can I share my perspective on this, though?

They've been heard; in return, they should be willing to hear you without confrontation.

4. Unreceptive dynamics

There are too many people talking and not enough people listening.

A good chairperson will ensure this doesn't happen, but there's not always a good chairperson. You can direct proceedings by asking someone: 'I'd like to hear what you think on this.' And you can stop people talking by saying: 'Okay, I'm clear on that.'

Sometimes people talk over each other when they fear not being heard at all, so make sure you're giving people the space and time to say what their views are even when you disagree with them.

5. Negative focus

The focus seems to be on everything that's going wrong and suddenly you feel entirely deflated.

Ease the focus away from the past and concentrate on the future.

Okay, I think we've got a full picture now. So...how can we move forward?

6. Zero common ground

You had a basic disagreement about causes of difficulties based on a huge gap of understanding and you just couldn't bridge the gap enough to forge a satisfactory plan forward.

If the gap in understanding is too big for you to bridge, you need help from the outside – someone who has experience of autism and the trust of schools, who can advise as a third party. More on that in Chapter 13.

7. Repressed feelings

You had strong emotions and you didn't want to shout or cry, so you closed off and never really expressed what was bothering you, as it seemed 'unprofessional'.

As we said earlier, the strong feelings that govern you are caused by the feeling that your child is unsafe, either physically or emotionally, and your protective instinct is natural and should be acknowledged.

Do express:

★ what you see at home, which may not be entirely visible at school

★ the causes of your concerns

★ your fears for the future.

8. Blame culture

Veiled hints took the place of direct accusations, leading to a focus on who was to blame for the situation to date and why.

If someone has outright pointed the finger, it's useful to redirect the conversation so that it's the *situation* that is tackled. This is far less emotionally fraught than blaming someone.

However, what to do when a person's attitude *is* the situation? That's coming next.

A NOTE ABOUT FACE-TO-FACE MEETINGS

We'd like to acknowledge that the reality for working parents might be that you won't be able to drop everything and visit your child's school. If you collect them, meeting half or three-quarters of an hour before pick-up can be convenient and very focusing. If that isn't convenient, virtual meetings are the next best thing and certainly less one-sided than an email.

Also, although it's not for us to dictate how people run their lives, it's often a good idea for parents to have an open discussion with employers about flexibility. There's an article about this in *AuKids* Issue 43 – 'The Juggling Act' (see Appendix 2: References and Resources).

TIPS FOR SCHOOLS
- Keep parents/carers informed.
- Make sure they know who to contact and how.
- Provide honest communication – there is no long-term benefit in providing anything but the truth.
- Listen to parents/carers – give them time.
- Try to avoid uncertainty or misinterpretation.

CHAPTER 13

WHEN SCHOOL TURNS SOUR

If your relationship with your child's school has broken down and you aren't feeling heard, there's a process that you can follow. Here is some useful advice about the process with some organisations that can offer you further support.

EDUCATION SUPPORT AND ADVICE

Every local authority in the UK has a Local Offer. This gives children and young people with special educational needs or disabilities and their families information about what support services the local authority is making available in their local area. Local authorities are responsible for ensuring that the Local Offer is available for everyone to see, not only through a website but through other means for those without internet access.

Look on the Local Offer website page to find your local special educational needs advice service, as well as other services that may help you in advising school on your child's needs.

Some local authorities have an Autism Team whose job is to assist parents and young people by visiting schools, assessing children's requirements and producing a plan of strategies and adaptations. If you've been assigned someone to support your family, they can visit you at home and discuss any problems you're encountering within the school system. They can then liaise with school and attend meetings with you as well. This can provide parents and carers with the necessary back-up and experience in order to instigate change.

If the school is not receptive to outside advice by experts and hasn't been listening to you either, you need to tackle the failure at the highest level within school before going any further.

THE SCHOOL'S GOVERNING BODY

If you feel that things aren't moving forward, a date-stamped letter to the headteacher and governing body SEND-link outlining your concerns and calling for a meeting is next on your to-do list.

You may also like to gather the relevant school policies. For instance, if a behaviour policy indirectly discriminates against your child by not allowing for flexibility, this may well be the source of the problem and needs to be pointed out.

It's a good idea to bring someone else to the meeting – a support worker who knows your child well, a social worker, the local authority's Autism Team representative or just a calm friend or relative to take notes.

A wonderful booklet written by parent Geraldine Hills, director of the Inclusive Choice Consultancy, has been written to help you understand school and the law. This fantastic guide is particularly helpful in explaining the process of getting an EHCP and making a complaint against the school. *A Parent's Guide to Disability Discrimination and Their Child's Education* is available to order in print or to download free of charge (see Appendix 2: References and Resources). Geraldine set up her consultancy as a result of discrimination against her own son at school, and she trains both parents and schools in the Equality Act 2010. As well as general advice about the complaints process, the book provides some sample complaint letters, too.

Schools will have their own procedures outlined on their website in an appropriate section or policy on how to action a complaint. Ask for any documentation you can't find.

The Information Advice and Support Service (IASS) offers help, advice and support in England for disabled children and young people, and those with SEN and their parents or carers. You can find your area's service on the Council for Disabled Children's website (see Appendix 2: References and Resources).

The National Autistic Society has published some helpful guidelines on resolving disputes with schools in England, Wales, Scotland and Northern Ireland – see Appendix 2: References and Resources for links.

THE INDEPENDENT PROVIDER OF SPECIAL EDUCATION ADVICE – IPSEA

If you have concerns regarding your child's EHCP, contact the SEN/EHCP team at your local authority.

IPSEA has details on its website about what to do if the content of your child's EHCP isn't being honoured. Its volunteers are legally trained and its website contains many downloadable guides on tackling problems. You can also contact them by phone or email.

Be wary of independent professionals who offer advice and support but are not appropriately qualified. Always work from recommendations and/or ensure they have appropriate professional membership before contracting anyone for paid work.

CHANGING SCHOOLS

Moving your child from one school to another is known as an in-year admission. You'll need to contact the local authority to find out about their in-year admission arrangements. Often, this can be done online through the local authority's website.

However, you may need to apply directly to the school if it's a free school, academy, voluntary-aided or voluntary-controlled school. In any case, it's a good idea to talk to your proposed school first and arrange a visit and a chat.

Helping children to adapt to changing schools

As we said in Chapter 1, having the news that they are going to a particular school 'dropped' on them from a height can make any child feel anxious, let alone an autistic one. The impact of this is significantly raised if they are facing a change of school.

Many autistic children may have an instinctive dislike of change and might therefore opt for the 'better the devil you know' approach. This can make convincing them that there's a better option out there fraught with difficulty.

Some advice for this particular situation: Please try to avoid dangling the notion of a change of school over a child's head if you haven't yet committed to the plan. Although you may be losing faith in a school's competency, it's not a great idea to sow the seeds of doubt about their provision in your child's head – with all the potential change this encompasses – before deciding for certain that it will happen.

What you can share is that you are working to do everything you can to make their school a better experience for them, talking things through to resolve difficulties, and that you are listening all the time to your child's views. If things aren't going so well, help them to create a list for you on what is going well and what isn't working for them.

We hope that you won't have to move schools, but if you do, research using our advice in Chapter 1. When you have a definite option in mind, have this conversation with your child:

What's working well at school?

What would you change if you could?

If someone could wave a magic wand and things would be better, what would change?

What makes you feel happy and okay?

What things do you wish *weren't* there?

Once again, using that collaborative approach with your child, you can sit down together and look at their wish list (rather than each other).

Remember how we talked about introducing new ideas earlier on in this book? Rather than imposing: 'I think you should go to...', you can now say: 'Hmm, I've looked at this wish list and I think it may be possible for us to make some of this come true? Would you like to know how? What do you think about this possibility?'

Due to uncertainty connected with change, it's a good idea to stop the conversation quite early, once the idea has been broached. Don't expect immediate agreement. Just plant the idea that there is a place where they might feel happier.

For the next conversation, return to them with their wish list, and show how when we look at new ideas, we balance up the pros and cons. For every wish they've shown, indicate a tick or a cross next to their current provision and a tick or a cross next to their proposed new provision. We can then see how evidence suggests there is a place that might be better.

There will be more anxiety – you need to be prepared for that. But it won't come as any surprise to you to know that the more visual information you can supply the better. All that groundwork we talked about in the earlier chapters will now stand you in good stead. Meeting a TA beforehand is also a great idea, and a gradual transition period during which a few hours are spent over the course of several half days will also work wonders in building their confidence.

Do be honest with your child. Explain that all change includes an element of uncertainty and what we call risk. Adults learn to weigh up risk by getting as much information as they can.

Appreciate that your child's trust may have taken a bit of a knock, and show that you understand this. However, you can also point out that people can learn a lot from unhappy experiences and that by using them, you've been able to make a more informed decision when it comes to a new school.

And, of course, once you know that a school is one that's open to collaboration and is flexible, you are very likely to have a good experience.

CHAPTER 14

THE AUTISM-FRIENDLY SCHOOL

Our Blueprint for the Future (If We Could Do Magic)

Throughout this book we've done our best to be realistic. We've acknowledged that the world isn't perfect and that the schools our children attend daily have difficulties that can sometimes be overcome by a good set of strategies combined with effective collaboration.

However, in order for any society to move forward, we have to know what 'good' looks like. Then, while we are still overcoming problems caused by our present systems, we can be planning for a better future – a future in which SEND isn't sidelined but becomes part of policy and planning at every level.

So, allow us to indulge ourselves in this final chapter with a dream of what we'd like mainstream schools to look like in the future. And, just to top it off, one example of where this is really happening.

The boxes in this chapter contain examples of daily practice from SENCo Lisa Spragg, who works at Hulme Hall School – an independent co-educational grammar school in Stockport. Thanks, Lisa, for sharing so many positive examples – and sorry we couldn't fit them all in!

1. INCLUSIVE TOP-DOWN CULTURE

Our autism-friendly utopia has expertise in SEND at the very top, creating an inclusive culture at every level. Think Blackpool – inclusion running through a school like a stick of rock!

2. FLEXIBILITY

The bottom line is that the academically able shouldn't be pressurised to the point where they are academically unable.

In our ideal school, parents and carers are given choices about how many subjects their autistic children take, so that timetables have suitable gaps for recovery from social and processing demands. Those gaps are used to focus on other aspects of their development that are equally as important – speech and language therapy, homework, self-regulation and meditation. It isn't the same for everyone; the beauty of the Saturation Model is that it doesn't have to be. Flexibility includes breaks for physical activity (not just sport) so that all pupils can focus better.

In Hulme Hall, there is enrichment support (in place of foreign languages on the timetable for some), to consolidate literacy and numeracy. This can run if needed all the way through secondary school. We find that small group work promotes confidence. A 'social thinking' group is run once a week at lunchtime for autistic students. We also have a homework club which helps some pupils who aren't comfortable doing work at home and see 'school as school'.

3. EXPERT TRAINING

All teachers in our autism-friendly school have up-to-date and regular training in autism, and education in autism is bespoke rather than an 'off the shelf' package. The training focuses on differences rather than disability and includes autistic testimonies. They share their own experiences of good and bad practice and the impact of both on them. Outside expertise is brought in to facilitate good understanding and practice.

We often engage the council's excellent Autism Team in work with the pupils in school and we facilitate the sessions as part of the school day. This is 1:1 or in a small group. We regularly ask for advice and they have given us full staff training in the past.

4. PEER GROUP TRAINING

Good-quality, immersive and interactive peer group training takes place, with autistic testimonies again part of that training. How does it feel to have sensitivity to environmental demands and difficulty with self-regulation, anxiety when faced with change, plus difficulties with auditory processing and social skills? Well, in our autism-friendly school, everyone knows how it feels – and understands what can happen as a result.

As well as peer group training, time within the curriculum is devoted to celebrations of individual differences and quirks, not purely concerning autism but *all* pupils.

Promoting an acceptance of difference is fostered early on during the journey here. Using CPSHE lessons (Citizenship and Personal, Social and Health Education) is good for this, or registration time where we can talk about a particular challenge someone might have. This is always done with parental permission.

5. REFLECTING AND HELPING CHILDREN TO REFLECT

At a great school, practitioners constantly reflect on their own contributions to challenging situations. They empathise with the young people they teach and have plenty of communication with them and their families. As a result, support is constantly improved. Teaching staff are genuinely curious about each new situation and use an individualised rather than a broad-brush approach to difficulties.

A restorative approach is in place here with that at the heart of the work that the pastoral team do. I think that giving your time to listen to the child's perspective is vital. We always make sure that parents are aware that from the perspective of the pastoral team, it is wellbeing that matters first and then if we get this right, the academic stuff usually follows.

6. SUCCESSFUL COLLABORATION

Great collaboration is ongoing – there are regular catch-ups and exchanges of ideas and strategies. Collaboration with autistic pupils also happens regularly, inviting their insights on how well school is meeting their needs and truly involving young people in all aspects of their learning and development.

Being involved right from the admissions process is helpful. We meet the parent during this time and absorb as much information as we can. We always remember the parent knows the child best. We work together to write plans and we work with the pupil to identify strengths, likes and achievements they are proud of. We also identify dislikes, what not to do and what works well. We do the same with the parent and then add information from external agencies. This helps de-escalation and is usually a good way of identifying stress.

For me it is all about getting to know the pupil. Taking the time to talk to them whenever the opportunity arises is essential. They then see you as approachable and this starts to build a positive relationship.

Our open-door policy is also something that works well here – it means that trust is built up and we can share what works for the individual. Sometimes parents just need to talk to us as much as the pupils do.

7. BULLYING POLICIES AND BUDDY SYSTEMS

Support from peers is encouraged through peer training. There are also systems to encourage a reflective approach after bullying. Buddy systems are in place to support pupils in making new friends, and out-of-school activities are inclusive, too, to encourage participation.

We offer our Enrichment Centre for eating lunch as a quiet space. This is supervised by staff and then when lunch is eaten there are many lunchtime groups (not just sporting) such as chess club, craft club, retro games club.

The weekly social thinking group runs with an emphasis on building friendships. Buddy systems help pupils to feel supported if they are feeling distressed first thing in the morning.

8. GREAT IN-HOUSE SYSTEMS

In-house speech and language therapists and educational psychologists in mainstream schools support both teaching staff and the autistic school population by providing guidance and support to enhance provision. Timetable gaps are used for therapy sessions, so that there is a focus on all-round development in combination with academic achievement.

9. PREVENTION RATHER THAN CURE

The Saturation Model is followed, ensuring proactive practice. This includes support for exams and being flexible around other forms of support and equipment, such as iPads for writing.

The school uses photos of places the pupils will visit and a time-line of activities is shared in advance with particularly anxious students so that they build up a picture of where they are going. Parents work with school to identify what might provoke anxiety. Sometimes school invites the parent to accompany (from a distance) if it's appropriate in younger year groups.

For trips abroad and the Duke of Edinburgh Award, there is careful collaborative planning and deployment of the right staff to be advocates for the young people. School staff always attend camping trips and training for the Duke of Edinburgh Award. Allocating key people is a huge thing for us here – we let the young person gravitate to who they prefer to instead of forcing it on them. This relationship is like a safety net for them, and we make ourselves available at unstructured times of the day.

10. COMFORTS ARE RESPECTED

There's an understanding of how difficult self-regulation can be for autistic pupils, and the positive and calming effects of familiar items, plus quiet time and space if and when it's needed.

> Pupils and parents put together 'Happy Bags' that include photos and other calming items which help promote good feelings. They are left in a wellbeing room for when the pupil needs a break. The school also encourages use of mindfulness packs including gorgeous pens and colouring.

11. RECOGNISING DIFFERENT LEARNERS

Teaching staff have enough autism awareness to be able to adapt, taking into account auditory processing problems as well as literal thinking and difficulties with abstract thinking. They're specific about what's needed from their pupils and able to adapt in order to get the best out of each one.

> I don't think I can underestimate the importance of our Pastoral Manager here – she advocates tirelessly for the pupils, and this is a full-time role here, she is available all day every day for whoever needs her (she is excellent at supporting staff, too). She also helps the whole staff team because of the relationship that she establishes with the parents of our vulnerable pupils.

SHARE THE INSPIRATION

Throughout this book we've shared examples of great practice. One message that we'd really love you to take from this book – be proactive. Help to steer the ship in a way that will guide it away from the rocks! Collaborate and communicate positively. Arm staff with the information they need to succeed. Keep in regular contact with them. Listen during times of conflict. Bring your home strategies to school.

With the advice in this book, you can foster a better understanding of your child within the school setting. And if enough of us do this, then our education settings will start to change for the better, having an impact on future generations.

What we wish for above all else is happier autistic children, growing into happier adults...and their well-informed peers growing into well-informed adults.

Best of luck from both of us!

Useful Charts

Interactive version of these charts can be downloaded from https://library.jkp.com/redeem using the code KDLUSUJ

④

Your checklist for choosing an inclusive secondary school – Page 1

Section 1: Pre-visit research	✓ or ✗ or ?	Notes	Score out of 10
Website – is inclusion mentioned?			
Anti-bullying policy easily available on website? If you can't spot it, ask about it at the visit.			
Photographs of SEND pupils or SEND work on website?			
Other SEND parents' views positive?			

④ **Your checklist for choosing an inclusive secondary school – Page 2**

Section 2: First impressions	✓ or ✗ or ?	Notes	Score out of 10
Who showed you around – did they have a senior role and plenty of knowledge? Was it a pupil/group of existing pupils?			
As a SEND parent, did you feel welcome?			
What sort of messages are conveyed to pupils through posters and displays around the school?			
Did you meet other autistic children?			
Did they listen when you told them your child's needs?			
Did they include your child in the conversation?			
Were other pupils welcoming to your child?			

Your checklist for choosing an inclusive secondary school – Page 3

Section 3: Meeting	✓ or ✗ or ?	Notes	Score out of 10
Did they show evidence of proactive practice in meeting different needs? Could they give examples?			
Did they listen to your child's views and show understanding?			

④ **Your checklist for choosing an inclusive secondary school – Page 4**

Section 4: Your questions	✓ or ✗ or ?	Notes	Score out of 10
Where can autistic children go at unstructured times if the playground is too much for them?			
If the lesson gets too noisy, what can they do?			
Do you provide peer group training in autism?			
Can my son/daughter be given extra time to get changed in PE classes? Is a separate changing area available?			
Can any changes to the timetable be made for autistic pupils – e.g. extra breaks or reduce number of lessons?			
What sort of adaptations does the school have?			
What sort of clubs do you hold at the school? Can a new one be developed if your child has a specific interest?			

⊕

Example of classroom tips chart compiled by parents and TA at primary school

Hurdles, stressors and opportunities	Why it happens	What we do
Saying 'no' rather than 'I'll try' to something new.	Trying something new feels threatening to him and very uncertain.	If he can be persuaded to give something a go for five minutes only, he usually enjoys it and there is a 'way out' if he doesn't, so he's happier.
Getting angry if something he likes suddenly stops.	Transition times are difficult for autistic children, especially if they are involved with something.	Let him know how long he has on an activity before it starts and give him a 10-minute and 5-minute warning before the end.
Sharing something.	Again, getting involved with something means it's quite hard to share. Open-ended timings are difficult.	Use a sand timer to show him and the other person in a visual way how much time they have left with an item. He can then see how much time he has until it's his turn again.
Getting annoyed or upset.	Can be because of overwhelming noise.	Easily distracted by jokes. When really upset, time to cool down in a quiet area. This is unusual.
Hard to build something out of his imagination from scratch.	Is quite a concrete thinker.	Will use his interests to build stories and scenarios. At the moment this is Skylanders Spyro game.
Worrying about time left.		Please let him know what time he will be collected.

④ **Blank classroom tips chart**

Name:

Hurdles, stressors and opportunities	Why it happens	What we do

Student passport template

Forename SURNAME OX1	Curriculum support faculty Student passport	Insert school logo
Date of birth: [date]		Last updated: [date]
Insert college/year	Faculty liaison: [name]	
Access arrangements Provide details of access arrangements, with a link to further information on usual ways of working. Insert photograph	**I would like you to know that:** . . This means that: . . . *Provide details of the diagnosed need(s), and what that means to the learner (as discussed). Make sure that this information is clear and useful to staff.*	**I find it difficult to:** . . . *Add specific areas that are difficult, with a focus on in-class learning but also practical challenges that staff need to keep in mind.*
It would support me if you could: . . . *Highlight teaching and learning strategies and practical support, as agreed in prior discussions.*	**I will support myself by:** . . . *Set out what the learner will do for themselves as part of the process. This may provide opportunities to link to other systems of reporting.*	
	Data and attainment information	
Additional support	*Provide details of the support you provide, such as SALT 2x30 sessions per week, in-class TA support or LEGO™ therapy once a week. Ensure this information is specific and quantified.*	

④ **Homework planner – example**

Homework	Deadline	How long it should take	How many days left?
Finish Maths exercise	8 November	30 minutes	7
Revise Science chapter on solids, liquids and gases	10 November	45 minutes 3 x 15 minutes	9
Read chapter of *Lord of the Flies*	4 November	20 minutes	3

Homework planner – blank [for laminating]

Homework	Deadline	How long it should take	How many days left?

References and Resources

Chapter 1: Finding the 'Perfect' Setting
References
Department for Education (2014) *The Equality Act 2010 and schools: Departmental advice for school leaders, school staff, governing bodies and local authorities.* Accessed 22/6/21 at https://assets.publishing.service.gov.uk/government/uploads/system/uploads/attachment_data/file/315587/Equality_Act_Advice_Final.pdf

Chapter 2: Transition Preparation
Further reading
Book
Elley, D. (2018) *Fifteen Things They Forgot to Tell You About Autism.* London. Jessica Kingsley Publishers.

Chapter 3: Preparing the Ground for Secondary School
References
Book
Dunn Buron, K. and Curtis, M. (2012) *The Incredible 5-Point Scale.* Shawnee, KS: AAPC Publishing.

Online
AuKids magazine (2016) 'If you're happy and you know it draw a face.' Issue 30, p.13. Accessed on 17/9/2021 at www.aukids.co.uk/aukids-issues-2029-1.

Morewood, G.D. (2014) 'Our effective alternative to IEPs' (student passports). *SEN Hub Magazine*, Optimus Publishing, pp.10–11. Accessed on 25/6/21 at www.gdmorewood.com/wp-content/uploads/2015/05/Student-Passport-article-Morewood-2014.pdf.

Blog article
Morewood, G.D. (2015) 'How to develop student passports – the movie.' The Optimus blog. Accessed on 25/6/21 at https://blog.optimus-education.com/how-develop-student-passports---movie.

Morewood, G.D. (2018) 'Revisiting the student passport' (includes new template). The Optimus blog. Accessed on 25/6/21 at https://blog.optimus-education.com/revisiting-student-passport

Further reading
Books

Huebner, D. and Matthews, B. (2005) *What to Do When You Worry Too Much*. Washington, DC: Magination Press.

Huebner, D. and Matthews, B (2007) *What to Do When Your Temper Flares*. Washington, DC: Magination Press.

MacKenzie, H. (2015) *Self-regulation in Everyday Life: A How-to Guide for Parents*. Ontario: Wired Fox Publications.

Mahler, K. (2015) *Interoception: The Eighth Sensory System*. Shawnee, KS: AAPC Publishing.

Chapter 4: Building the Foundations for Collaboration
Websites

Orkid Ideas – www.orkidideas.co.uk

Chapter 5: Comfort Among the Commotion
References
Book

Beardon, L. (2020) *Avoiding Anxiety in Autistic Children*. London: Sheldon Press, an imprint of John Murray Press, p.57.

Blog article

Morewood, G.D. (2020) 'Why constant consistency matters: Emotional regulation as a foundation for learning.' The Optimus blog. Accessed 22/06/21 at https://blog.optimus-education.com/why-constant-consistency-matters-emotional-regulation-foundation-learning.

Journal article

Fixers (2018) 'Feel Happy on the Spectrum Report.' Public Service Broadcasting Trust. Accessed on 12/05/21 at www.fixers.org.uk/feel-happy-fix/feel-happy-on-the-spectrum-autism/the-report.php.

Further reading
Books

Smith, R. and Barron, P. (2020) *The Art of Weeing in the Sink: The Inspirational Story of a Boy Learning to Live with Autism*. County Durham. Carpet Bombing Culture.

Toeps, B. (2020) *But you don't look autistic at all*. Rotterdam: Toeps Media.

Online articles

AuKids magazine (2018) 'Senses Working Overtime.' Issue 41, pp.10–11. Accessed on 17/9/2021 at www.aukids.co.uk/aukids-issues-4050.

Websites

Headspace meditations – www.headspace.com

Myatt and Co, Films for Teachers and Leaders, Gareth D. Morewood and Debby Elley talk on joint working, parts 1, 2 and 3. Available (paid access) on 15/6/21 at https://myattandco.com/authors/debby-elley-gareth-morewood.

Chapter 6: Jumping the Barriers: The First Six

References
Journal
Dodge, R., Daly, A., Huyton, J. and Sanders L. (2012) 'The challenge of defining wellbeing.' *International Journal of Wellbeing 2*, 3, 222–235.

Books
Toeps, B. (2020) *But you don't look autistic at all.* Rotterdam: Toeps Media.
Vermeulen, P. (2012) *Autism as Context Blindness.* Shawnee, KS: AAPC Publishing.

Further reading
Books
Cain, S. (2013) *Quiet: The Power of Introverts in a World That Can't Stop Talking.* London: Penguin.
Elley, D and Houghton, V. (2020) *The Ice-Cream Sundae Guide to Autism.* London: Jessica Kingsley Publishers.
MacKenzie, H. (2015) *Self-regulation in Everyday Life: A How-to Guide for Parents.* Ontario: Wired Fox Publications.
MacKenzie, H. (2019) *Teacher's Guide to Autistic Behavior: What, Why and How to Help.* Ontario: Wired Fox Publications.
McGraw, P. (1999) *Life Strategies: Doing What Works, Doing What Matters.* New York, NY: Hyperion Books.

Online talks
Cain, S. (2012) 'The Power of Introverts.' TED talk. Accessed on 21/6/21 at www.ted.com/talks/susan_cain_the_power_of_introverts.

Websites
Orkid Ideas – www.orkidideas.co.uk
Picturepath – www.mypicturepath.com
Our Boards – http://ourboards.co.uk
The Curly Hair Project (Alis Rowe) – www.thegirlwiththecurlyhair.co.uk

Chapter 7: Jumping the Barriers: The Next Six

References
Beardon, L. (2020) *Avoiding Anxiety in Autistic Children.* London: Sheldon Press, an imprint of John Murray Press, p.49.
Elley, D and Houghton, V. (2020) *The Ice-Cream Sundae Guide to Autism.* London: Jessica Kingsley Publishers
Schneider, R. (2016) *Making Sense: A Guide to Sensory Issues.* Arlington, TX: Future Horizons.

Further reading
Online articles
AuKids magazine (2018) 'The Autism Friendly Classroom.' Issue 38, pp.10–11. Accessed on 17/9/2021 at www.aukids.co.uk/aukids-issues-2029-1.
AuKids magazine (2020) 'Homework: How to Win the Battle Without Making Enemies.' Issue 47, pp.8–9. Accessed on 17/9/2021 at www.aukids.co.uk/aukids-issues-4050.

Websites
KanbanFlow – www.kanbanflow.com

Chapter 8: A New Vision: The Saturation Model
References
Journal

Morewood, G., Humphrey, N. and Symes, W. (2011) 'Mainstream autism: Making it work.' *Good Autism Practice Journal 12*, 2, 62–68.

Book

Gray, C. (2001) *My Social Stories Book*. London: Jessica Kingsley Publishers.

Online article

Morewood, G.D. (2014) 'Case study: Sensory audit using assess, plan, do review.' The Optimus blog. Accessed on 22/10/2021 at www.gdmorewood.com/wp-content/uploads/2019/01/INCLUVISION-3L.pdf.

Further Reading
Books

McCann, L. (2018) *Stories that Explain*. Hyde: LDA.

McDonnell, A. (2010) *Managing Aggressive Behaviour in Care Settings: Understanding and Applying Low Arousal Approaches*. Chichester: Wiley-Blackwell.

McDonnell, A. (2019) *The Reflective Journey*. Peterborough: Book Printing UK.

Online article

AuKids magazine (2012) 'Maps of the Social World: Using Social Stories to Help Your Child Navigate Their Way.' Issue 15, pp.10–11. Accessed on 17/9/2021 at www.aukids.co.uk/blank-page-1.

Morewood, G.D. (2019) 'Understanding emotional regulation in the context of whole school inclusive systems.' *Incluvision*, January–April, pp.6–9. Accessed on 22/10/2021 at www.gdmorewood.com/wp-content/uploads/2019/01/INCLUVISION-3L.pdf.

Morewood, G.D. (2019) 'Autism and inclusion: The Saturation Model explained.' *Optimus Education*. Accessed on 22/10/2021 at https://my.optimus-education.com/autism-and-inclusion-saturation-model-explained.

Special Children magazine (2016) 'Social Stories for Children with Autism.' Issue 228, pp.30–33. Accessed on 28/6/21 at https://reachoutasc.com/resources.

Online film

Studio 3 (2019) Gareth D. Morewood on the Saturation Model. YouTube. Accessed on 21/6/21 at www.youtube.com/watch?v=qXTBY-WH9JA.

Websites

LASER training – www.studio3.org

Reachout ASC – www.reachoutasc.com

Chapter 9: Tackling Bullying Together
References
Book

Batten, A., Corbett, C., Rosenblatt, M., Withers, L.T. and Yuille, R. (2006) *Make School Make Sense – Autism and Education: The Reality for Families Today*. London: National Autistic Society.

Journals

Beaumont, R. and Sofronoff, K. (2008) 'A multi-component social skills intervention for children with Asperger syndrome: The Junior Detective Training Program.' *Journal of Child Psychology and Psychiatry 49*, 7, 743–753.

Campbell, J.M., Ferguson, J.E., Herzinger, C.V., Jackson, J.N. *et al.* (2004) 'Combined descriptive and explanatory information improves peers' perceptions of autism.' *Research in Developmental Disabilities 25*, 4, 321–339.

Campbell, M., Hwang, Y.-S., Whiteford, C., Dillon-Wallace, J. *et al.* (2017) 'Bullying prevalence in students with autism spectrum disorder.' *Australasian Journal of Special Education 41*, 2, 101–122.

Morewood, G., Humphrey, N. and Symes, W. (2011) 'Mainstream autism: Making it work.' *Good Autism Practice Journal 12*, 2, 62–68.

Humphrey, N. and Hebron, J. (2015) 'Bullying of children and adolescents with autism spectrum conditions: A state of the field review.' *International Journal of Inclusive Education 19*, 8, 845–862.

Robertson, K., Chamberlain, B. and Kasari, C. (2003) 'General education teachers' relationships with included students with autism.' *Journal of Autism and Developmental Disorders 33*, 2, 123–130.

Further reading
Online articles

AuKids magazine (2020) 'Inside Angle: Life through a Lens' (Alfie Bowen). Issue 49, pp.12–13. Accessed on 17/9/2021 at www.aukids.co.uk/aukids-issues-4050.

Contact (2019) *Dealing with Bullying: Information for Parents of Disabled Children.* Accessed on 21/6/21 at https://contact.org.uk/wp-content/uploads/2021/03/dealing_with_bullying.pdf.

The National Autistic Society (2006) 'B is for Bullied: The experiences of children with autism and their families.' Accessed on 21/6/21 at www.autismtoolbox.co.uk/sites/default/files/resources/B_is_for_bullied%20National%20Autistic%20society.pdf.

Book

Elley, D. (2018) *Fifteen Things They Forgot to Tell You About Autism.* London: Jessica Kingsley Publishers.

Websites

Alfie Bowen photography – https://alfiebowen.photography
Bullies Out – www.bulliesout.com
Kidscape – www.kidscape.org.uk

Chapter 10: Making Friends
References
Online articles

AuKids magazine (2020) '"Smile Like You Mean It": How Should We Teach Social Skills?' Issue 46, p.14. Accessed on 17/9/2021 at www.aukids.co.uk/aukids-issues-4050.

AuKids magazine (2021) 'My child is desperate for friends. What's the best way she can make them? She feels so isolated.' Issue 50, pp.6–7. Accessed on 17/9/2021 at www.aukids.co.uk/aukids-issues-4050.

Further reading
Online articles
AuKids magazine (2013) 'The Safety Net.' Issue 21, pp.10–11. Accessed on 17/9/2021 at www.aukids.co.uk/aukids-issues-2029.

AuKids magazine (2018) 'Ask the Experts Friendships Special.' Issue 41, pp.6–9. Accessed on 17/9/2021 at www.aukids.co.uk/aukids-issues-4050.

Websites
Autcraft autism-friendly Minecraft play – www.autcraft.com

Spectrum Gaming – www.spectrumgaming.net

Further reading
Books
Jones, H. (2014) *Talk to Me: Conversation Strategies for Parents of Children on the Autism Spectrum or with Speech and Language Impairments.* London: Jessica Kingsley Publishers.

Shaul, J. (2014) *The Green Zone Conversation Book: Finding Common Ground in Conversation for Children on the Autism Spectrum.* London: Jessica Kingsley Publishers.

Shaul, J. (2020) *Your Interests, My Interests. A Visual Guide to Playing and Hanging Out for Children on the Autism Spectrum.* London: Jessica Kingsley Publishers.

Chapter 11: When Conflict Is on the Horizon
Online article
AuKids magazine (2016) 'From a Black and White World to Thinking in Colour – How to Improve Flexibility of Thought.' Issue 33, pp.14–15. Accessed on 17/9/2021 at www.aukids.co.uk/aukids-issues-2029-1.

Books
Elley, D. (2018) *Fifteen Things They Forgot to Tell You About Autism.* London: Jessica Kingsley Publishers.

Kerstein, L. (2014) *A Week of Switching, Shifting, and Stretching: How to Make My Thinking More Flexible.* Shawnee, KS: AAPC Publishing.

Chapter 12: Handling Disagreements
References
Journal
Morewood, G. D. and Bond, C. (2012) 'Understanding parental confidence in an inclusive high school: a pilot survey.' *Support for Learning 27*, 2, 53–58.

Further reading
Online article
AuKids magazine (2019) 'The Juggling Act.' Issue 43, pp.14–15. Accessed on 17/9/2021 at www.aukids.co.uk/aukids-issues-4050.

Chapter 13: When School Turns Sour
Further reading
Books

Hills, G. (2017) *A Parent's Guide to Disability Discrimination and Their Child's Education*. London: Lulu.com

Hills, G (2020) *The Equality Act: An Easy Guide to Disability Inclusion in School for Educators*. London: Lulu.com. (Free to download from www.inclusivechoice.com/books)

Websites

IASS (Information, Advice and Support Services) – https://councilfordisabledchildren.org.uk/information-advice-and-support-services-network

IPSEA (Independent Provider of Special Education Advice) – www.ipsea.org.uk

Council for Disabled Children – https://councilfordisabledchildren.org.uk

Inclusive Choice Consultancy (training on equality and the law for parents) – www.inclusivechoice.com

National Autistic Society, Working with your Child's School to Resolve Differences:
- www.autism.org.uk/advice-and-guidance/topics/education/resolving-differences/england (England)
- www.autism.org.uk/advice-and-guidance/topics/education/resolving-differences/northern-ireland (Northern Ireland)
- www.autism.org.uk/advice-and-guidance/topics/education/resolving-differences/scotland (Scotland)
- www.autism.org.uk/advice-and-guidance/topics/education/resolving-differences/wales (Wales)

The School Run – www.theschoolrun.com/changing-your-childs-school

Chapter 14: The Autism-Friendly School: Our Blueprint for the Future
Further reading
Books

McDonnell, A. (2019) *The Reflective Journey*. Peterborough: Book Printing UK.

Online articles

National Autistic Society (2020) 'Social Stories™ and Comic Strip Conversations.' Accessed on 21/6/21 at www.autism.org.uk/advice-and-guidance/topics/communication/communication-tools/social-stories-and-comic-strip-coversations.

Websites

LASER training – www.studio3.co.uk